There's
Always
Tomorrow

There's *Always* Tomorrow

EMILIE DEFREYNE

G2 RIGHTS LTD
KENT

G2 rights ltd

There's Always Tomorrow
Copyright © Emilie Defreyne 2012

First edition published in the UK in September 2012
© G2 Rights Limited 2012
www.G2rights.co.uk

eBook Edition ISBN :978-1-909040-87-8

G2 Rights Ltd, Unit 9 Whiffens Farm,
Clement Street, Hextable, Kent, BR8 7PG

To my friends
whose love and support have made this book possible,
and to at least one person for whom I hope
my recollections will have given hope and encouragement.

Contents

Prologue

Early on a grey frosty February morning in 1998 I stood watching as the cold deep water of the river carried ever further from me the ashes of my late mother which a few minutes earlier I had scattered upon the surface. A late winter leaf fluttered down to join the grim procession.

I am numb with cold and the weariness of loss. I stare blankly as the last physical evidence of the woman who gave me life disappears into the low hanging mist, just as I had stood some fifteen years earlier with her by my side bidding farewell to my father.

They are both gone now, and I stand truly and completely alone in my grief and the personal torment that dominates my life.

Although it was with a heavy heart that I turned away to face another day, I vowed then that if I ever found a way through the unhappiness surrounding me I would write a book the overwhelming aim of which would be to give hope and encouragement to those in despair, together with the belief that no matter how hopeless and desperate today may seem – there's always tomorrow!

Quiet Beginnings

How many of us, I wonder, have idly watched a leaf journeying downstream, marvelling as it negotiates unexpected hazards so to continue its travels almost as though destined by the forward flow of the water to encounter and conquer further difficulties and periods of calm before finding that ultimate place of rest and peace.

Life seems to run on similar lines, and in the narrative that follows I have tried to balance the undoubted pleasures of life with a desire to give hope to those who have found the darker times difficult to negotiate. If just one person who reads the following account of this particular leaf's journey through life so far derives some comfort, hope and reassurance that however bleakly and desperately events unfold there is a way through to better times, then the aim of this book will have been achieved.

For those whose faith explains adversity and provides guidance, comfort and courage, I have every respect although not envy. We are given a life and it is up to us how we use that life. Mistakes of all kinds are inevitable but we must be accountable for our actions and where possible learn from errors and move forward better able to make wiser decisions. The absence of a faith has never worried me; maybe I have one as yet unacknowledged. The strength and ability to deal with much that life so far has dealt me comes from trying to do my best honourably with the life I have been given, and secondly – and by no means least – from the truly wonderful gift of friendship.

It is to my remarkable friends who have believed me and believed in me that I owe so much. Without their unstinting love, loyalty, kindness and support in countless ways I doubt that I would have survived. To them, therefore, with immense gratitude I have dedicated this book.

Somewhat contrary to the title of this the first chapter, my arrival into the world on a spring day in 1947 was far from conventional; nearly two months premature, I was born in an ambulance valiantly making its way towards University College Hospital against the tide of an excited Cup Final crowd. I was only the second surviving infant born to my mother from five confinements. Noting that I weighed in at under two pounds with my knees joined together, and sported a shock of bright red hair, the midwife tried to console my mother with the comment, 'Well, she may not be much to look at but at least she has plenty of character!' Whether my mother was indeed comforted or not and whether the judgement has proved true I cannot say, but I would settle for it as an epitaph!

My brother, some six years older, had been in poor health and my doctor parents, after a great deal of consultation with their many colleagues and considerable heart-searching themselves, made what must for them have been a momentous decision. They abandoned quite well-established and extremely promising careers in London and moved to rural coastal Essex, where it was hoped the clean fresh sea air would benefit my brother's health.

All this happened, of course, before the introduction of the NHS, and at that time the usual way to become a general practitioner was to buy an existing practice and to build it up through personal endeavour. Remuneration was based on patient numbers, so with no guaranteed backup, or such arrangements as group practices, the new doctors had to quickly make themselves known as hopefully agreeable, trustworthy and competent. Then by way of word of mouth their patient numbers would increase. It also followed that a successful practice with a healthy number of patients on the list in an affluent area would be far more expensive to buy than a practice in a more remote part of the country which had been allowed to run down.

With the financial implications of purchasing and funding a practice, a home and bringing up two small children, my parents had no choice but to opt for the latter. Having secured the practice and acquired a large but also run-down farmhouse in an auction sale, they moved to Essex – and so perhaps I became an original Essex girl!

Even as a small child I think I realised and accepted without any sense of rancour or discontent that with the workload they had to carry, my parents would not have that much time for us. In no way were we neglected, except perhaps in terms of time devoted to us, but that time was just not available and therefore for my part I felt no resentment. Sadly, perhaps because he was older and therefore needed a different level of interaction, and had received considerable attention when little due to his indifferent health – or maybe because we are all intrinsically different – but for whatever reason, my brother rebelled quite early on, and I remember feeling sad and puzzled as to why he could not settle and find solace. With hindsight, I look back now with even greater sadness, knowing that he in his way was calling for help and my parents in their way were doing everything they thought would assist him. I learnt much later in life just how much my father wanted a son to whom he could feel close and just how much my brother had yearned for a father to whom he felt he could relate.

No parenting class will ever provide adequate preparation for that most complex of relationships. As the one guides, the other grows – sometimes in harmony, sometimes in conflict. All but the most unworthy parents do their best – some better than others, through skill or chance – the vast majority constantly striving to do the best they can in the circumstances. The most precious gift a parent can give their child is their time, and never more so than today in a world filled with the numerous and increasingly available advantages and attractions of technology. These can certainly amuse and entertain, understandably tempting the busy parent to delegate responsibility for providing that vital personal relationship to the amazing array of entertainment options available.

Happily, my brother's health improved, but with the sense of underlying resentment he harboured I remember an uneasiness always present, even when obvious efforts were being made to help him. A tall, strong, good-looking lad, temptations of all sorts became available and the feeling of distance seemed to make it inevitable that he would leave home sooner rather than later. With seafaring in my father's family, and his service as a surgeon commander during the war, my father pulled as many strings as he could and managed to secure a position for my brother with a reputable shipping line, in the hope that with his free spirit and love of the sea he would find his way and eventual happiness.

Before all that happened, however, life was not all doom and gloom by any means. Even as small children, we had to contribute to necessary routines and I remember clearly my main early morning duty was to clean all the shoes, and I found my father's large footwear particularly challenging, my whole arm being needed to fill the shoe so I could use the brush with the other. All disciplines such as bed making, tidying rooms, laying tables, washing up etc., were accepted as quite normal. Frequently, one or other parent would have been out on a call during the night, but morning surgery and the calls of the new day would still require attention. Initially, the expense of additional premises being out of the question; surgeries were held in the house which meant that half the sitting room became the 'waiting room', another front room became the 'consulting room' and what had been an old scullery became the 'dispensary'. The hallway was to be as little used as possible during surgery times as contact between ourselves and patients was not encouraged.

I have so many memories of those days, for example, my dear brother one Sunday night before going to bed standing at the top of the stairs leading up from the hall announcing plaintively that he felt sick. Almost simultaneously and before any steps could be taken to avert disaster, he vomited a plentiful helping of previously consumed tomato soup all the way down the stairs, walls and carpet. To this day I can see the mixture of emotions showing in the faces of my parents. Concern for my brother mingled with the prospect of spending most of the ensuing night restoring the hall from what had in seconds become a passable film set for a massacre back to a respectable entrance hall ready to receive patients for Monday morning surgery!

My parents' apparent ability to work all hours in those days was always a source of amazement to me and never more so than at Christmas time, as the tree and paper chains miraculously appeared between our going to bed on Christmas Eve and coming down on Christmas morning – after, of course, we had emptied the stockings so carefully set out at the end of the bed. I can only conclude they fell into bed just in time to get up again, always assuming they had not been called out. Presents were precious: the stocking contained an orange, a walnut, chocolate money in gold foil and maybe half a crown (12 1/2p). In the beginning, I was also given a sugar mouse but, showing early signs of a later commitment to vegetarianism, I concealed these among my clothes, only to have an army of ants discover them later in the year – much to my mother's understandable annoyance – and I was thus banned from receiving sugar mice again. In addition, under the tree would be the 'main present', and that was that. When I see the volume of gifts received by children today I thank my parents wholeheartedly for the real 'magic' of Christmas that we were lucky enough to enjoy. It may not have been seriously religious but it was certainly special.

Financial considerations, together with my parents being constantly on call, meant we had no family holidays away and very few outings at all. However, with over two acres of garden to enjoy, and the close proximity of coastal backwaters, there was plenty to keep us occupied. East Anglian winters can be hard, but equally the summers were usually long and warm. When little, my brother and I were obliged to find our entertainment within the confines of our large garden, which we did happily.

So often my champion in those days, he rescued me from frequent mishaps. I was very small (apparently a search for 'Small' usually had to be mounted several times a day) but this never deterred me from embarking on none too sensible adventures. On one occasion I was discovered by my brother stuck in deep mud, sinking rapidly, with mud beginning to ooze over the top of my wellingtons. My knight in shining armour plucked me bodily from my wellies and carried me to safety. By this time fear had turned to tears, so my brother sat me on his knee and we had a good laugh at the pair of little wellies just peeping above the surface of the mud.

Our nearest neighbours were a family employed mainly working on the land, but they also had fingers in other pies and generally considered to be a 'dodgy' lot. The house and garden were very run-down with piles of rubbish and bits all over the place. They had one son, who for some reason was the constant butt of his father's bad temper. In fact, the constant stream of invective hurled at the poor lad morning, noon and night at full volume both worried and annoyed my parents. As children do, my brother inevitably picked up some of this language, particularly as he had been told not to – some things never change!

One day I was seen to fall head first off a swing onto the concrete patch which had been put there to protect the grass from scuffing feet. When my parents reached the scene of this drama, they found my brother cradling me in his arms, endeavouring to soothe me with the words, 'You darling little bastard, please don't cry.' Not knowing whether to laugh or cry, my parents first made sure my head was intact. Then they took my brother aside and gently explained that this was no way to address his little sister!

Our parents' treatment of us when we were ill was excellent but very clinical, which with hindsight was completely understandable. My mother was academically brilliant, for instance, when studying medicine (which in itself was rather ahead of her time) she felt the need for a diversion, so she took a degree in Ancient Greek to help pass the time! She wrote numerous papers on different medical topics and later became involved in the pioneering stages of cancer treatment, to name but a few of her many achievements. My father was no means a slouch in the intellectual department either. His seafaring father had wanted him to follow a career in engineering rather than medicine, so he first qualified as an engineer and then as a doctor. To this he added a partial training in law to pursue a career as a coroner, working closely with and being highly thought of by no less than the then high-profile coroner, Sir Bentley Purchase. All that of course came to an end with the move to Essex.

When we needed the benefit of their combined medical expertise, they never let us down. Witness the move to Essex for my brother. In my own case, when presenting with a burst appendix at under two years old, it was solely my mother's stubborn confidence in her diagnosis that ultimately just saved my life.

With small ailments, however, the approach was quite different, with the result that it was much wiser to keep quiet. Any mention of a sore throat, for instance would always be met with an instruction to go to bed, and someone would come up after evening surgery, if there was time. Experience taught us to be careful not to mention problems before tea, unless we really did not want any food, as the reasoning was that if our complaint was worth mentioning we were not well enough to eat, and as there was no heating in the bedrooms (a fire might be lit, but rarely) it was more prudent to say nothing and stay by the range in the kitchen. Because of this, I think we quite often attended school with childhood ailments that kept most of our contemporaries in bed for days, and for my part I was often met with the extraordinary observation, 'You can't have a cold, your parents are doctors!'

Always content within their medical world, my parents never really felt the desire or need to socialise, and in fairness within the limited rural community in which they practised the opportunities to do so were very few.

However, it was essential that they made themselves agreeably known whenever possible if the practice was to thrive, and an instance in this regard was to lead to one of those sayings unique to family life, the root cause of which is often a mystery to others. My father was walking along a path behind some cottages and espied a woman hanging out her washing. He knew her name but she was not then a patient. His greeting of, 'Good morning, Mrs Herbert,' met with an unexpected response. Without turning round or pausing in her work, the good lady answered in a perfectly civil tone 'Arseholes to you.'

One could be forgiven for suspecting some ulterior reason for this retort, but on the contrary Mrs Herbert later enlisted and was a patient with my parents all the time they were there. We were left to assume therefore that somehow this was regarded as a normal 'courtesy', and for ever after in the family if something occurred to us as inappropriate, rude or out of kilter, we would just grin and say, 'Good morning Mrs Herbert!' – as I say, doubtless to the puzzlement of others.

This lane also provided the setting for another little cameo witnessed by my father on his way home from a late evening call. A gentleman in the same line of cottages kept geese; those familiar with these delightful creatures will know they are every bit as efficient as any guard dog and equally as inquisitive, but on occasions very quiet. The rear boundaries of these gardens often included a five-barred gate, as did this one, and against it on this particular evening were leaning a courting couple. Liberties as such were not taken so freely then, so when the girl felt a very determined nip on that part of her bottom squeezed through the gate she was definitely not amused. When despite her protestations the avian offence was repeated, if anything more passionately, she flounced off dismissing the pleas of innocence from her beau. One way or another that path seemed connected with bottoms!

Although we lived very close to the tidal backwaters when we were very little, unsupervised access to these was forbidden and visits to the more formal beaches of, for example, Walton-on-the-Naze were at a premium, only happening occasionally with my mother while my father held the fort.

This changed, however, owing to an understandable debt of gratitude felt by a family to my mother. At this time, the menace of polio was in its early stages, and with its initial symptoms being not dissimilar from those of influenza, it was yet another instance of my mother's exceptional skill that she detected the very early onset of polio in this couple's elder son, averting almost certain paralysis or even death.

Desperate to show their gratitude, an arrangement emerged whereby my parents secured a beach hut at Walton on the understanding that it was unreservedly for their family's use, but when convenient they would also take my brother and me. The family played their part to the full, and I have many happy memories of those excursions.

I have slightly misled my patient reader when I say we had no holidays away – in fact, we had one. Disaster is perhaps too strong a word to describe those few days but I do not recollect the event with any delight. Despite this meticulously planned break in all our routines I do not recall any gleeful anticipation, quite possibly because we almost resented an interruption in our well-ordered establishment. My brother was at an age where he was easily bored and made it quite clear he would infinitely have preferred to be somewhere else; I picked up on this and so we set off in less than holiday mood. All the usual contingency plans for an absence had been painstakingly sorted out, the most important of course being the engagement of a locum to run the practice.

Our holiday lodgings were dirty, very cramped and situated next to a large town clock that reliably chimed loudly on the quarter-hour, it rained non-stop, my brother sulked and I fell into a duck pond, so it was with a united resolve that holidays were obviously not all they were cracked to be that we thankfully made our way home… only to find the police waiting for us.

It turned out that the charming young locum doctor to whom my parents had entrusted their livelihood was on the run, having found acting as a short-term locum around the country an extremely effective way of staying one step ahead of the various pursuing county police forces. While there, he had apparently discharged his duties well, so no real harm had been done, and as children we found this to be by far the most exciting aspect of the whole holiday. The nature of his wrongdoings was never explained to us, but the whole episode certainly put paid to any further goings away.

Very occasionally a neighbouring but distant doctor would stand in. This necessitated the local telephone exchange having to do odd things with the lines for calls to be redirected, and it seemed to take weeks for things to return to normal. This was irritating as the practices were some considerable distance apart. Few though they were, these opportunities to do something as a family were precious. Having no television and very restricted access to the 'wireless', all concepts or knowledge of what lay beyond my own boundaries came by necessity from books, which in turn fuelled a young fertile imagination. Apparently my abilities to read, write, walk and swim came almost simultaneously, each in its own way aiding my development and leaving me from a very tender age with strong emotional and practical self-sufficiency – attributes for which I was later to be truly thankful. A drawback of this almost total reliance on books was that certain events in my young life left me either terrified out my wits – or completely underwhelmed – when completely the opposite effect was intended.

The first of these was on my one and only visit to a pantomime made possible by one of the aforementioned stand-ins. The panto was *Dick Whittington* and of course the cat was played by an actor. I was able to contain my apprehension at this life-sized cat so long as it stayed on the stage, and I was also somewhat reassured that no one else in the audience appeared concerned. However, to my absolute horror, at the end of the panto, just when I was becoming more reconciled to the idea that this potentially dangerous creature never strayed from the stage, it leapt down among the audience and began to hand out sweets! Furthermore, it was making its way inexorably towards me. No longer able to control the rising tide of terror I let out a piercing scream and fled the theatre in tears, pursued by my bemused family, who had happily assumed I had been enjoying myself. To her eternal credit, the actress who played the cat took the trouble to find us, took off her costume head and knelt down beside me – and so a tiny introduction to the theatre was made.

On Sundays, although my parents were still 'on call', there were no surgeries and the day became a pleasant ritual; all things being equal, my father read to us for an hour or so in the evenings. He was an excellent reader and chose widely and wisely from the classics, comedy, plays, fiction and non-fiction. Among the many titles of course came *The Jungle Book* and the *Just So Stories* and many other tales involving fantastic adventures and animals, and this in its turn led to my being completely under-whelmed when I should have been awestruck.

I had some trouble with my eyes as a child and was taken by my mother to see one of her old chiefs in Harley Street. She had decided that in an effort to make the ordeal more acceptable it should be combined with a visit to London Zoo, followed by tea at DH Evans. For me, the concept of size when it came to animals was drawn almost entirely from reading with no physical comparisons. Therefore, I knew elephants were large – really, really large. On approaching the elephant enclosure my mother, with something like triumph in her voice, announced, 'Well then!'

I realised that I was expected to respond favourably and quite differently from the feeling of disappointment that I felt. Was this it? I thought, having imagined the beast to be some ten times bigger. I enquired timidly if it was a baby elephant, but no; the first of many a childhood illusion was gone. I was however hugely impressed with the hippo that appeared to spend the whole time with its truly enormous mouth wide open. Passers-by threw in sandwiches and fruit and were periodically rewarded by the animal swallowing the accumulated donations, only to reopen its mouth for the next instalment... There seemed no concern on the part of the keepers that anyone would feed the beast anything harmful – how times change!

Tea at DH Evans, however, certainly lived up to expectations. I did not know what a Knickerbocker Glory was, but as the ingredients shown on the menu looked so inviting, I readily agreed to opt for that alone as it was quite expensive. I think my mother's motives for limiting me were twofold – admittedly the expense, but also the size: it was enormous, and so beautifully created that I can safely say I have not seen its equal since. It was so tall and I was so small that I had to reach up to hold the spoon, much to the amusement of those at surrounding tables, who then (according to my mother) were entertained by the mixture of determination and sheer unalloyed enjoyment with which I tackled my first Knickerbocker Glory!

Apart from these occasional expeditions further afield, life very much revolved around the routine of the practice, which was quite an education in itself. Even before I could write I was empowered to answer the telephone and learnt to remember quite long messages and numbers and develop a feel for what was genuine or urgent.

An effort was made for us to eat as a family whenever possible, and when we were old enough tea was usually postponed until after evening surgery. Although we were in no way repressed, the pattern then was for children seldom to speak unless invited to do so. Tea was often the first opportunity my parents had to discuss the day; the topics were frequently not for the squeamish but nevertheless often very amusing. Of necessity, we therefore acquired an inbuilt sense of integrity and discretion, together with a commonsense approach to many aspects of medicine in its widest sense. This basic sensible and undramatic approach, unconsciously acquired, has stood me in good stead over the years when faced with having to deal with, be involved in and advise in distressing situations.

It is fair to say that most small, insular communities have their fair share of eccentrics, the more so before travel was so easy. Before the introduction of the welfare state, with its wealth of advantages and disadvantages, the structure of a rural community was quite hierarchical but in fact worked very well, or at least it seemed to where we lived.

My parents were good doctors and worked hard, gaining through their efforts the respect and affection of the community as a whole. Looking back, much of this was due to their perception and willingness to adapt to what was around them. For example, the grand lady who lived in an enormous house on The Green demanded almost daily visits to appease her hypochondria – more importantly, she was very happy to pay for this, knowing full well that much of that money would in fact subsidise other patients who could not pay. Payment was often made in kind. Living in mainly a farming community, my parents were often given produce instead of money, and together with a thriving orchard and vegetable garden of our own we were blessed with no shortage of good fresh food.

One such benefactor to us on the food side was a local dairy farmer called Mr Robinson, whose wife had a lifelong battle with her weight, being sorely tempted by a constantly available supply of fresh bread, butter and cream. However, my mother had become rather alarmed at the piling on of the pounds, and had gently suggested one or two diets. I should explain here two things: firstly, in the village my father was always Doctor and my mother Dr Elizabeth; and secondly, and more important to this anecdote, although Mrs Robinson was a thoroughly likeable person, nobody would have described her as beautiful – except of course presumably Mr Robinson!

One morning, Mr Robinson had occasion to see my father in surgery on a matter pertaining to himself, and at the end of the consultation, on rising to bid Mr Robinson goodbye, my father expressed the hope that Mrs Robinson was keeping well. At this Mr Robinson sat down again, fixed my father with an earnest look and said, 'We're so grateful, Doctor, for the trouble that Dr Elizabeth has taken with my wife's weight – we really are – but Doctor, you know my wife, she's not gorgeous, really she's not.

Please, Doctor, please do tell Dr Elizabeth my wife's not at all gorgeous.'

Wishing in no way to hurt the good man's feelings, my father managed to keep a straight face, reserving his laughter for later when he relayed the message to my mother.

Eccentrics come in all shapes and sizes, and a mark of the respect in which my father was held was the night 'the Martians' landed. On some wasteland there lived an old man in a caravan. Neither his background nor his means of subsistence were ever discovered. He drank heavily and this, together with other problems, had meant my father visiting him quite regularly, which he did willingly. Although obviously very eccentric, there seemed no real malice in the old man until very late one night when, by then very drunk and wielding a shotgun, he declared war on anyone coming near him in the belief they were Martians. The local bobby (a personage so sorely missed these days) telephoned my father requesting help and advice. On arriving at the scene, my father called up an ambulance from the asylum in Colchester. Then he told everyone to stand well out of sight as he intended to go into the caravan and bring the gentleman out. PC Roley was none too happy at this, or the prospect of my father incurring serious injury, but my father insisted and all ended as happily as it could. My father managed to negotiate his way into the caravan and persuaded his patient that the scene was indeed surrounded by Martians – no point in trying to argue that issue – but that my father had managed to procure a safe vehicle for their escape, and so with a quick dash to the waiting ambulance and expert help, the drama was over.

My father was typically unabashed by all the fuss and I always remember him saying that all good psychiatrists must be a little mad themselves to be able to do their job well. Perhaps I would have substituted 'unstuffy' or 'imaginative' in place of 'mad', but I knew what he meant.

Another alcoholic lived alone down by the backwaters in an old tumbledown house, and he too was visited periodically by my father. The conditions were extremely squalid but the old man was the very proud possessor of one luxury, namely, a telephone, and so it was that he was able to telephone for assistance in the middle of the night. The scene that greeted my father was as bizarre as the explanation.

The old man had drunk himself into a stupor, and on waking saw at the end of his bed what he thought in the candlelight to be the fingers of two hands, presumably belonging to someone about to spring onto the bed and attack him. Reaching stealthily over the side of the bed, he picked up his shotgun and, fortunately then still being none too focussed, shot at his own toes. With a wry grin he admitted to my father that it had certainly sobered him up. Fortunately, no great harm had been done, so my father tidied him up – and the old man insisted that my father stay and share a drink with him to celebrate! Out of kindness and probably just to keep an eye on him, my father sat a while with him and then emerged into the cold light of another new day.

As time went by, and presumably finances became a little easier, changes did occur. For a while, premises were rented in the village for the surgery, and then a purpose-built extension was added to the farmhouse incorporating a waiting room, toilet and consulting room – the dispensing still being done from the house. All this was done at my parents' expense. Admittedly, it released the family home back to the family, but it was also engineered for the benefit of the practice in general and was welcomed with gratitude by the patients.

My mother, an avid gardener when time permitted, always arranged the garden bordering the path to the new surgery with seasonal flowers, and she was therefore intrigued when after surgery one morning my father returned to the main house, clutching a bunch of flowers which looked suspiciously like our own. The bearer of this gift was a dear little lady who had long harboured a yen for my father and who was one of what was known in the family as a 'season ticket holder' – meaning that it would not be uncommon for her to attend every surgery run by my father over the course of several days or weeks. We set up a watch from the main house, and sure enough, every time Mrs Hubbard visited my father she gathered as many flowers as available from our garden to give to him.

During school holidays my father would often take me with him on his rounds, which was both informative and fun. The highlight of these outings was always to 'The Hall' – a vast old house set in magnificent grounds which had become a rehabilitation/nursing home. Whereas I never entered The Hall itself, I was allowed complete freedom of the grounds while my father was attending to his duties. The gardens were a wonderful mixture of large formal lawns, flower beds and huge, long-established trees. There were several large lakes linked by delightful waterfalls and many less formally managed areas where wildlife thrived. I found that by sitting still and quietly, gradually a whole different world would unfold before me of frogs, newts, fish, dragonflies, beetles, moorhens and of course the inevitable ducks and swans. It was the most idyllic of settings and reinforced in me an already growing fascination and respect for life in all its forms.

The signal for my return to the car was one hoot on the horn, and woe betide me if I did not appear quickly. The establishment was run by a pleasant, large, round-faced Matron with lovely wide-set brown eyes, and I always politely thanked her before we departed. After one such visit, our next call took us along the coastal road, which at one point bordered a field full of Jersey cows. Essex being mainly arable, cattle were not that common-place so we would often stop at the gate and pull up bunches of grass from our side of the gate to give them, as even cattle seem to think the grass on the other side is always greener!

This day the 'leader' of the herd, who had become a particular favourite, being a beautiful looking beast, very gentle and always the first to appear, sidled up to the gate. Perhaps because we had only just left The Hall, my father turned to me with a chuckle saying, 'Look, here comes Matron!' And so she was known thereafter. On subsequent visits to The Hall when saying my farewell, I was always amused at the undoubted likeness between the two.

I have mentioned that when small I was very small, and this was due to a poor appetite which was in turn due to chronically enlarged tonsils and adenoids, so it was decided I should be admitted to Colchester General for their removal. Although a very routine procedure, the prospect was a frightening one for me, with no experience of being 'away from home'. On a pre-op visit, a promise of jelly and ice cream as part of my post-operative care was made in order to dispel my obvious apprehension.

Sadly, on the day, and suffering the inevitable vomiting as well as a very sore throat, my misery was compounded by the arrival of a very austere Sister obviously not privy to any promise of ice cream and jelly. She presented me with a doorstep size piece of well done toast with the brusque instruction to eat it as it would 'get rid of the slough'. I had been brought up to do as I was told and to respect my elders and betters, but I knew I could not eat the toast – but I also knew that it had to disappear. I managed to conceal not only this offering but subsequent ones behind the metal backrest of the bed and so a day later, very frightened (and hungry), I was collected and taken home.

No discovery had been made by then, and I of course said nothing of my 'crime', but I knew it would come to light and then what would happen. My fertile imagination, well grown through reading, knew no bounds. By the time a few days had elapsed I had worked myself into such a state that on anyone coming to the house I would make myself as scarce as possible. I was convinced that a prison sentence for me and probably the entire family would be the very least punishment to be meted out to me and those I had implicated by association. In our busy household it took a while for my abnormal behaviour to register fully, but after a couple of weeks my parents were becoming alarmed at my apparent lack of post-op progress and state of continual anxiety.

Very gently, my father coaxed me to confide to him the cause of my despair. Eventually, accompanied by uncontrollable sobs, I owned up to my terrible wrongdoing, which I had convinced myself would lead to the most dire retribution for me and those I held dear. Needless to say, my father quickly reassured me and dispelled my fears. Whether or not he said anything to the hospital I never knew, but I remember him putting his arm round my shoulder and saying, 'Do you know, dear, I think I would have done exactly the same! So why don't we go and ask your mother whether sometime soon we can have jelly and ice cream for tea, to make up for you missing out in hospital?'

One instance when a quiet word in the right quarter averted trouble was the instance of the 'mothball man'. So far I have made little or no mention of my formal education, partly because it was wholly unremarkable. Although involving a long bus journey, as my brother was that much older and thus able to keep a brotherly eye on his little sister, our initial schooling was by way of private tuition in a neighbouring town. From this, my brother went to school in Colchester, whereas I, having failed the eleven-plus, went to a secondary modern, again involving a long journey by bus.

It came to pass that nearly every morning a gentleman sat next to me on this journey. At eleven years old, anyone over thirty years seemed old, so to me he seemed an older, quite friendly although very inquisitive gentleman. He questioned me closely about all sorts of aspects of my life and family. One evening, when having tea after evening surgery, my father asked me if I had had a good day at school, and I happened to mention 'the nice gentleman who always sat next to me on the bus'. At this my father pricked up his ears and asked me a little more about this nice gentleman, what sort of questions he had been asking and what he looked like. I gave as good a description as I could and commented that he always smelt strongly of mothballs.

I thought no more of the matter but noticed after a day or so that the mothball man had disappeared. I learnt years later that my father had sought out the previously mentioned PC Roley, only to find that the 'mothball man' was well known to the authorities as being a bit of a nuisance, so a discreet word was sufficient to nip the situation in the bud. With the good community awareness that existed in those days, I imagine many other similar situations were quietly dealt without the weight of bureaucracy now employed, which so often misses the target anyway and is inevitably followed by highly expensive public enquiries whose recommendations are usually ignored and seldom implemented.

I remember the feeling of disgrace which accompanied my failure of the eleven-plus as my parents were already beginning to transfer to me their expectations of high achievement which they had previously hoped my brother would fulfil.

I have good memories of my time at the secondary modern, and it certainly served to broaden my outlook socially if not academically. I was never as brilliant as my mother, few aspiring to her intellectual heights, but tended to plod through whatever was put before me. I became more acutely aware that it was not just my future I had to worry about, but that I was also expected to achieve where my brother had not, which became later a very onerous burden, and one with hindsight I might have been wiser to challenge more vigorously than I did; but again, times were different and dissent was not viewed favourably.

There was one small instance where the hurly-burly, rough and tumble and no-holds-barred topics of conversation of a secondary modern completely outshone my mother's expertise in the most astonishingly way. I have no idea how my father tackled the question of the facts of life with my brother, but in my case this duty was left to my mother. The attentive reader will probably have gathered that my father was as far as I was concerned the more approachable parent. My mother doubtless loved me, but she did not suffer fools gladly, so failure to grasp a discipline or instruction the first time inevitably led to scorn or sarcasm. These are very destructive to a growing mind trying hard to please, and certainly discourage requests for explanation or further information.

Therefore, having been summoned to see her as she had something important to tell me, when I was aged about nine, there followed what must rank as one of the most misleading statements ever made, and which I can remember word for word to this day: 'Men have twiggies and they can make you pregnant so be careful.' And that, as they say, was that and I was dismissed.

To say that I was confused was an understatement, and for many a long year I looked at trees and men, wondering how on earth this worked, as I had obviously gleaned a few clues with my love of nature and through books. Some hilarious albeit humiliating conversations with my more streetwise contemporaries at the secondary modern straightened things out very quickly!

To some people, my childhood would come across as unusually lonely, particularly after my brother had left. However, by then old enough to wander, I accepted and revelled in this freedom, relishing the opportunity to observe and understand all around me. Probably, my happiest days would be spent in the summer holidays. Morning duties performed, away I would go with a book, my beloved teddy bear and some fruit from the garden, my return not expected before tea. So it was that I would spend long hours understanding the tides, exploring rock pools, watching the seasons unfold, lying in long grass searching the clear blue sky for skylarks – learning so much without realising, and all the time gaining a respect for and understanding of life, death, silence and peace. So much of this reinforced my ability to function within myself and thus be content, which was to prove so invaluable later.

Maybe in an effort to emulate my parents' doctoring skills, I was always eager to help anything in trouble and became quite successful, for example, in nurturing abandoned fledglings to maturity and ultimate freedom. While I was a toddler 'helping' my mother in the garden, I had become so concerned that earthworms would get cold that I would gather them into my gloves for warmth. Needless to say, they were later diplomatically returned to the soil.

We also had our fair share of pets, the main one being an Old English sheepdog called Kim. Apart from a few instinctive chases after local cats, it quickly became apparent that Kim was not as energetic as he should have been. The local vet diagnosed a genetic heart problem and so Kim never ventured further than the garden – the boundaries of which, to be fair, he guarded well. He was gifted with a wonderful temperament except towards dustmen and window cleaners, and with careful management and care he lived to a ripe old age, his days in fact ending after we had left Essex.

We also had a rabbit which tragically caught that most vile of diseases, myxomatosis, presumably through contact with a wild rabbit. Even though the wild rabbits posed a threat to crops, the local farmers were so sickened by the suffering caused to the rabbits that they would often go out at night to shoot those affected and helpless in order to end their misery.

I was allowed to keep mice, although with one exception they were confined to a disused but substantial stable block; it served as a garage and workshop and stood some distance from the house. The exception was one little fawn mouse, called unsurprisingly Fawny, who stole all our hearts. Very gentle, alert and intelligent, he could be allowed complete freedom in the yard at the back of the house and would happily cooperate in the numerous games devised for him. He also amazingly shared my father's passion for Gorgonzola cheese, although we had to limit his intake on health grounds – the mouse, that is, not my father!

However, not all Fawny's friends were so gentle. I was thrilled one day to find a brood of baby mice had been born (despite my parents' efforts to segregate the sexes), but joy turned to horror when careful inspection later that day revealed Blackie (a black and white big bruiser of a male) in the act of eating the last offspring! Deciding that Blackie's temperament was probably better suited to the wild, where his aggressive nature would improve his chances of survival, we released him.

Tragically, the remainder of the colony did not survive long after that event. Answering a night call one frosty winter's night, before leaving the stable block my father checked the mice and the adequacy of their bedding and all was well. During his absence there must have been a freak drop in temperature. Inspecting them again on his return, he made the grim discovery that they had all frozen to death, including of course my beloved Fawny.

Billy was my brother's budgie and was much loved by us all. Central heating not existing in earlier times the kitchen was definitely the place to be, and here Billy's cage was located. Despite hours of patient tuition, the most Billy every uttered in human terms was 'Squidgy Billy', but he was a delightful little character. He would be transported into endless trances of delight, either at his own reflection or cooking noises such as bubbling or sizzling or, in his ideal world, the two together.

Billy was frequently allowed out of his cage to stretch his wings and generally explore. His two favourite landing places were a yellow drum of Vim powder and the table, which was always covered by a rather threadbare faded crimson chenille cloth. The latter delighted Billy and he would spend as much time as he was allowed strutting around the cloth extracting as many of the remaining threads as he could, and we never had the heart to stop him so obvious was his enjoyment.

My mother had nine stepbrothers born to her father's first

wife. He was widowed a second time dramatically when his wife died giving birth to her first child – my mother. Amazingly, we only met *one* of her stepbrothers. Some had died in infancy or were casualties later in the war, and one was an engineer killed in Malaya when a dam burst. The uncle with whom we had any contact at all had moved to the USA and become a naturalised American. He sent wonderful parcels to us containing all sorts of goodies the like of which neither my brother nor I had ever seen before.

On two occasions he came to see us, the first visit being in Essex. He was a tall, balding man with an extremely gentle unassuming manner, and I remember him with great affection. One evening during his stay, as was the custom, we allowed Billy his hour of freedom. On being released he flew his usual circuit ending up on the Vim drum preparatory to his swoop to the tablecloth. Whether by design or accident he instead landed on Uncle Eddie's head. Digging his sharp claws into the shiny pink surface, he then began carefully to pluck out the fine hairs that grow on even the baldest of pates. With tears rolling down his cheeks, Uncle Eddie bravely resisted the temptation to brush Billy off for fear of hurting him. We responded to my uncle's cries for help and Billy was returned to captivity.

Fortunately or unfortunately, my brother was away when Billy had to be put to sleep. The trouble began with the startling revelation that Billy was in fact a lady budgie, this becoming apparent when she tried to lay an unfertilised egg. My parents managed to deal with this, but sadly when it happened again the resulting prolapse was beyond repair. It was decided that after I had gone to bed my parents would put Billy to sleep by means of cotton wool copiously soaked in ether. Apparently due to neither of them relishing the task, soaked wads of cotton wool were passed back and forth until they were more in danger of anaesthetising themselves than the unfortunate Billy. Eventually, however, the deed was done and Billy was at peace.

I have enjoyed this love of animals and life in general throughout my life and am immensely grateful that I had the opportunity to develop a part of me in which I could find a personal sanctuary of peace and confidence, however bleak my actual physical and emotional circumstances. This personal haven was gloriously enhanced on reaching adulthood by discovery of the arts, a hitherto unknown world to me except in the form of literature. Although ridiculed during my marriage for this interest as either being 'poofy' or 'a dreadful noise', classical music in particular has given me strength and courage almost in equal measure, I would imagine, to that of a fervently held faith.

I have made reference to my much loved teddy bear who was my constant companion as a child. His name is Edward and he was originally my father's childhood teddy, this being authenticated by a very faded photograph taken in 1913 of my father with his mother, Edward, and maid! Edward very nearly met a most undignified end being discovered by my mother with his head in one Sainsbury's brown paper bag and his body in another, awaiting collection by the refuse men. So rescued in the nick of time he was 'restored' by my father, who as well as reuniting head and body also replaced his growler and re-stuffed him with some of my mother's silk stockings. The operation complete, my father then closed the wound, and Edward to this day proudly 'bears' a most exquisite surgical scar!

As so it was that Edward became and has remained throughout my life my most faithful companion and confidant. Bears have played an extraordinarily important part in my life, of which more later, but suffice it to say at this stage that where I went Edward went, and all the joys and troubles of my childhood were shared with him.

Not having many toys, those we had were precious, and apart from Edward I also had and still have a velvet rabbit and a sausage-shaped sheep, plus an owl reputed to have belonged to my mother's maternal grandmother. Their potential value is immaterial as I would never part with any of them. I did also have one doll but certainly not of the cuddly kind. Dolls never really appealed to me, but this one was different. Being made of that peculiarly flexible post-war rubber, its head and limbs squeeze-fitted into appropriate holes in the torso. I discovered that at bath time if I filled the doll with water and then squeezed it as hard as I could the effect was most pleasing. I could usually manage to thoroughly soak most adults within range, the head being particularly effective. Needless to say, my parents did not share my sense of achievement, so 'dolly' was frequently confiscated!

I have dwelt long – not too long I hope for my patient reader – on anecdotes from my childhood, as it is from childhood that we take the core values then acquired forward into adulthood. Logically therefore our conduct in adult years is inextricably linked to the platform our childhood has provided.

My parents had worked very hard over the years to build a thriving practice and had gained respect and affection in the community. The introduction of the National Health Service and the welfare state in general proved to be the undoing of much that had been so painstakingly achieved. As is so often the case, the minority undermined so much that had been carefully planned to benefit the majority. My father, in particular, viewed the future with grave apprehension, and sadly I have seen many of his predictions come true.

After a few years of trying to wrestle with the new, they agreed they could no longer reconcile their vocation with what was occurring.

Just two instances that I myself witnessed are examples of the changes of behaviour which saddened and appalled my parents and strengthened their resolve to leave general practice.

Night calls were not infrequent but sensibly were made in cases of emergency. To my father's dismay he was telephoned in the middle of the night to attend an 'aching toe'. He enquired how long this ache had been present and was further dismayed to be told a few weeks. Not unreasonably, my father suggested the patient attend surgery the following morning, only to be informed that by the rules of the welfare state he was entitled to a call from the doctor anytime day or night, and if my father failed to do his duty he would be reported to the executive! I don't know how the matter was resolved but I know the huge harm it had done.

I have mentioned that as time progressed my parents, at their own expense, had built a surgery wing to the house. All went perfectly well until 'entitlement' became something approaching a national hobby, apparently extending to getting anything for nothing. So it came to pass that not only did magazines disappear from the waiting room, but also the toilet rolls – and on one occasion the toilet seat – left the lavatory, followed eventually by one of the chairs in the waiting room, so the remainder had to be screwed to the floor.

The sense of disappointment and disillusionment felt by my parents can only be imagined.

Of all the professions, medicine must undeniably be the hardest. The lawyer has time to consult his reference books and colleagues before arguing his case, and now with the absence of capital punishment mistakes are capable of remedy. The engineer can calculate with the benefit of time and instruments and plans can be counterchecked for accuracy before a brick is laid. The doctor however must keep all his accumulated knowledge at his fingertips; he never knows the problem that will face him, so he must be able to act quickly and decisively, often in difficult circumstances knowing a mistake can cost a life.

My father was the most compassionate of men, but about this time I can remember him once trying to explain to me why he would not in the 'new' world stop and offer his help unless and until called upon to do so in his official capacity. I can understand his reasons now; society seems today to revel in 'the blame game', and with litigation assuming the status of a fashion accessory only the bravest are going to stick their necks out.

So it was that my parents took another momentous step in their lives and left all they had built up to pursue the remainder of their medical careers in a different direction.

From Essex to Surrey

The decision to move having been made, my parents' efforts were naturally focussed on the future, and I watched in silent misery as preparations for our departure gathered momentum. I understood in some measure the reasons for our leaving and I sympathised, but the prospect of leaving behind the only world I had ever known filled me with anguish.

Our move took us to the Sussex town of East Grinstead and the contrasts were startling. Gone were the flat landscape, scattered housing and wide open spaces, to be replaced with hills, wooded areas and the bustle of living close to a thriving town. Most painful to me was the absence of the sea, and to this day I treasure every opportunity to return and walk by the water's edge feeling again that sense of home and belonging. Maybe because seafaring is in my blood, or because it formed such an intrinsic part of my childhood – whatever the reason – for me to sit looking at the sea at any time of year never fails to restore calm and resolve (in equal measure).

My parents, on the other hand, immersed themselves quickly in all that needed attention, and reference to our previous existence was usually ignored. To them, Essex had been a period in their lives from which they had decided to move forward, whereas for me it seemed almost a betrayal for those precious years and memories to be abandoned without so much as a backward glance.

My father had taken a post as a Medical Officer with the Army, whose barracks were temporarily located in Sussex pending a move to Surrey a few years later. My mother secured herself a position within a team pioneering the treatment of cancer, and with her usual intensity and ability she soon became an influential force in the development of both radiotherapy and chemotherapy.

The vexed question of my education also had to be addressed

again and my failure at eleven-plus level came back to haunt me. The grammar school would not entertain any attempt at O levels without setting me back a year, but this did not equate with my parents' ever growing expectations for my future. Eventually a convent was found that would, provided I passed an interview satisfactorily, allow me to sit examinations within a timescale acceptable to my parents.

I was duly taken for my interview and a tour of the school with my parents. A convent and nuns were a new experience for me and I remember feeling apprehensive, some of the more Dickensian institutions of which I had read as a child coming alarmingly to mind.

However, I was accepted, and as we stood in the drive saying our farewells the Mother Superior, a tall, gaunt, austere nun, bent forward to shake my hand. She gave a slight smile at which point to my utter amazement her false teeth dropped onto the gravel between us. Quite ignorant of the correct etiquette in such circumstances and wondering whether it represented some sort of initiative test for aspiring pupils, I bent down retrieved the dentures and handed them back to her. Never taking her eyes from my face or changing her expression she took them from me and popped them back into her mouth as though nothing out of the ordinary had occurred.

As the school was in a convent, religion formed a large part of its ethos, although in fairness it was never unduly forced upon me. However, I was expected to attend any parts of the daily routine involving religion, and these times set aside for spiritual enrichment provided me with ideal opportunities to catch up with unfinished work, with the result that I was frequently punished for irreverence. I arrived with no faith and left equally barren in that respect but at least with an adequate level of academic achievement.

Religion aside, the transition from secondary modern to convent was intriguing. Many of the pupils at the convent had spent most of their lives in this extremely sheltered environment with a resultant almost hysterical fascination with the opposite sex and a perturbing lack of ordinary common sense. Their childhoods too had been unusual in a different way, and I often wonder what became of some of them.

The education provided was adequate but again sadly with no enthusiasm for the arts, so my schooling proceeded again almost entirely on academic lines. Mathematics had never been my strong point and this was almost certainly the reason for my eleven-plus failure. With O levels approaching, my parents were called in to discuss which subjects I should take and it was decided much to their annoyance that it would be a waste of an examiner's time for me to sit mathematics, and that I should take biology instead, as at least it was a science subject. I was quite happy with this and my parents were somewhat appeased by the assurance that it would provide a sufficient base for the level of achievement they expected of me later.

Although my parents were now no longer on twenty-four-hour call, they both quickly became very involved in their new jobs with the result that provided they were satisfied that I was studying as much as possible I was left much as before to my own devices.

I had possessed little as a child and apart from my bedroom furniture, personal clothes and books, few tangible reminders of my past had come to Sussex with me. Needless to say, however, my beloved teddy bear, Edward, and his little band of friends had done so, although sadly, two other toys did not make the journey with me; my parents considered their inclusion inappropriate. The first of these was not surprisingly my little rubber dolly, mentioned earlier, and the second was a splendid little railway set.

Despite the busy lives they led in Essex my father in particular had always tried to find some time to do things with us.

These attempts at joint ventures usually involved my brother, as my father was desperate to build a closer relationship with him hopeful of dispelling those feelings of unrest and rebellion which beset his son, to which I have referred earlier. Together they made numerous ships from balsa wood, but the master achievement was the construction of a model railway entirely occupying a small anteroom upstairs in the old farmhouse and to which when I was small only supervised access was allowed. I have always been fascinated by miniature objects and it was therefore a treat to be lifted up to marvel at the miniature world thus created and the ingenuity that had been used. We always teased my father that there seemed nothing he could not do with a penknife and a nail file, these becoming known in the family as his universal tools!

However, it did slightly rankle with me that my brother should have so much time lavished on him, and so it came to pass that as one of my main Christmas presents I was given my own railway set. Although no rival to my brother's, it nevertheless gave me endless hours of pleasure and in its own way was ingenious. About two feet in length and battery operated, it comprised a figure of eight track cut out from metal under which was a sheet of felt which vibrated on a lever being moved. The rolling stock consisted of a little engine and three little carriages, all with felt on their undersides. On placing the engine or coaches onto the vibrating track they set off at high speed either backwards or forwards depending on the nap of the two pieces of felt when contact was made. Although there was nothing much besides a tiny platform and signal box at the crossover in the middle, there was a lift-off cutting at one end and a lift-off tunnel at the other. Enormous fun could be had inventing endless situations involving dramatic collisions, chases and escapes. In some ways it provided similar entertainment to that of dolly, but sadly with neither surviving the move I was left to hope that whoever acquired them derived as much pleasure from them as I had done.

If I have given the impression that my father ignored me then I am at fault, and one particularly fond memory I have of him is that in Essex after most evening surgeries (when, I now realise, he must usually have been exhausted), he would take the trouble to come up to see me in bed and make up a bedtime story. To have read from a book when that tired would have been challenging enough, but he would lie next to me on the bed and invent the most wonderful tales. Having got comfortable and warm it was not uncommon for him to fall asleep, whereupon in my impatience to hear the rest of the story I would dig him in the ribs to wake him up! The stories usually involved three characters called Bashy, Mugglewhump and Moldiwarp, but in earlier days had featured a little train called Smutty. It was therefore with some pride one day at school that I proudly announced that my daddy told me smutty stories at night. Fortunately, the world was a nicer place then, and my father's reputation remained unsullied.

Our dear Old English sheepdog, Kim, of course also came with us, but Sussex was to prove his final resting place. Never a well dog, we had kept him as fit as possible, and it was my duty to attend to his grooming, feeding and general welfare each day. It was difficult to discern any lessening in his energy because he had never been that active, and equally with his huge volume of hair any gradual weight loss was difficult to detect. However, when he started to vomit regularly and failed to respond even to my efforts to hand feed him minced food we knew the time had come. Even to this day – and sadly with experience later of attending dogs at that most painful time of parting – I am sure they know and even welcome the end of their suffering.

With Kim gone and my brother's visits home being only rare and regrettably always tense occasions, it was with Edward as my ever faithful confidant that I approached the future.

I was bought a bicycle as my first Sussex Christmas present, it being decided that as the convent was only some three miles away this would be the best means of transport there. Whether I could ride a bicycle or not was never questioned; fortunately I could, and so the road to eventual independence had begun!

The town was (and still is, as far as I know) home to a hospital famed for its extraordinary achievements in the field of plastic surgery. Its expertise and that of its leading surgeon, Sir Archibald McIndoe, became legendary during the war when dealing with the appalling injuries suffered in conflict. Accidents and injuries occur in peacetime too, and the surgeons' skill was still in great demand and I'm sure still is to this day.

Sometimes at the weekend I would be commissioned to cycle into town on some errand or other, and although I had no money of my own would happily spend an hour or so wandering around looking at the shops before returning home. It was on one of these outings that on turning a corner I was confronted by a man 'without a face'.

Although startled, somehow I knew I must not show it and instead I smiled. The face that was no longer a face belonged to a man in his mid-twenties whose features had been reduced to two holes for his eyes, two tiny holes for his nose and a gap for his mouth; apart from that he had no hair, rudimentary ears and skin painfully thin and stretched. Yet the look of gratitude in those sad eyes in response to my little smile broke my heart. No words were exchanged, but on returning home I told my father what I had seen and how it had affected me.

By dint of discreet enquiry within medical circles, it transpired that the young man in question was an Eastern prince who, in despair at being forced into an arranged marriage rather than choosing his own bride, had attempted suicide. The bungled attempt had left him with his life but with no face. In addition, as his culture forbade suicide, he had been disowned by his family, so alone he faced months upon months of agonising surgery in an effort to rebuild not only his shattered features but also his life.

Our stay in Sussex spanned a couple of years or so and after that initial encounter I often saw the young man in the town, and although we never spoke we always smiled and I watched in awe as his face was painstakingly rebuilt over that time. The amazing skill required and the pain that must have been endured to achieve a more acceptable face than that which I had originally seen were truly remarkable. On one of the last times I saw him, his mouth now complete, he gave me a real smile and I saw a tear track its way down his new face. I knew that soon I would be leaving, and I wondered if he too was facing a new future. I often wonder what happened to him and fervently hope that he found true love and happiness.

The end of my father's interim assignment signalled our next move, this time to Surrey. Fortunately, it came at a convenient time for my mother, and she took the opportunity of a post also as a Medical Officer with the Army, to be based near my father.

For me this move was much less daunting. I had always known our stay in Sussex was to be short-lived and it had provided me with a useful stepping stone from childhood to adolescence. I had reconciled myself to there being no going back and had grown to accept that home had to be where you were at any particular time. I will not deny, however, that my thoughts often harboured a yearning for the sea, the salt tang in the air and the feel of sand and water between my toes. Growing up and seemingly endless study contrived to push such feelings into the background.

My mother had arranged things so there was a gap between her assignments, whereas my father's carried almost straight over, and in view of this it was decided that my mother and I would go to Surrey for a few days to acquaint ourselves with the area. While the prospect of accompanying my mother was not in itself a problem, travelling any distance in a car with her was distinctly alarming.

As far as driving was concerned both my parents were entirely self-taught, as during the war in certain circumstances no test was required. In my father's case all was well, whereas with my mother this lack of formal training had resulted in a most unusual attitude to motoring. Her philosophy seemed to be that provided she knew where she was going that was enough, and such things as road markings, signs and indeed to a large extent other road users were to be regarded rather as nuisances put there deliberately to thwart her progress. Added to this, she had a complete lack of empathy with the mechanics or performance of a car, often sitting with her foot hard on the accelerator, obviously expecting some movement before remembering the little matter of gear selection, with the inevitable result that eventually the car would leap forward or backward and stall – much to her surprise and intense irritation!

In her defence, at the time when we were there rural Essex had few main roads and traffic was very light. Also, such was the esteem in which my parents were held that PC Roley would have needed serious reason to question my mother's capability to drive, or probably anything else for that matter. Of necessity, my parents had to have a car each. To my knowledge my mother never drove my father and he always insisted she drove the sturdier of the two vehicles, a Ford V8 Pilot known affectionately as 'The Warrior'. It was the driving of this larger vehicle that probably saved her life as when negotiating a narrow blind bend she collided with an Eastern National single-decker bus, the resulting impact effectively slicing away the entire off side of the car. Alighting from what remained of the Ford, she approached the obviously shaken bus driver demanding to know his name, to which he replied

'William Shakespeare.' To this my mother retorted furiously 'And I'm the b— Queen of Sheba!'

As my long-suffering reader will have guessed, the poor man's name was indeed William Shakespeare. The exact apportionment of blame was never determined, no action ensued and bizarrely the episode only seemed to confirm my mother's contempt for other users of the road, together with a somewhat misplaced confidence in her own abilities.

At one point on our visit to Surrey I remember all too well how she drove straight over clearly marked stop lines across a busy main road, coming to an abrupt halt in the road opposite. She turned to me, saying, 'Don't tell your father I did that.' It was as though she had some inkling, but within her intellectual world felt no need to bother with the more mundane aspects of living. Later this was to leave her quite vulnerable, as she seemed to distance herself even more from reality and common sense. Apparently, this is no t uncommon in highly intelligent people – hence the proverbial mad professor!

She made a statement to me once again within the context of a driving incident which probably best illustrates this curious dichotomy in her character.

On returning to her car after a clinic she found she had been blocked in by another car belonging to a fellow medic. Instead of locating her colleague and asking him to move his car, she proceeded to try and unpark hers. Her efforts were witnessed by the other doctor, but before he could reach the scene she had managed to quite badly damage the front of his vehicle. At the sight of this he was understandably furious and I suspect some-what puzzled. The long and short of it was that my mother could not or would not admit she had been at fault, and there followed an exchange of letters upon which she sought my advice. I went as gently as I could through the sequence of events in the hope that logic and common sense would prevail, and an abject apology and offer to pay would conclude the matter. However, my mother stubbornly refused to accept any blame, standing by her assertion that 'if he had not parked there I would not have hit him', and expressed serious doubts as to my legal expertise in failing to see the validity of her argument. In the theatre I think it is deemed inadvisable to act with children or animals, and similarly a caveat could be attached to the legal profession: don't act for friends or members of your family!

Although useful, our reconnoitre of the area proved inconclusive, so my parents decided to rent a furnished house to give themselves more time before purchasing a property of their own. The rented house was quite large, comfortably furnished and included a washing machine and a television – two items which my parents had always considered unnecessary and too expensive. So it was that as a family we were slowly, albeit reluctantly in the case of my parents, being pulled tentatively in a more modern world. Despite one or two slight mishaps with the washing machine it was soon embraced with enthusiasm, as was the television set, and I will always remember my father's delight at *The Magic Roundabout*, which became obligatory viewing before the evening news bulletin.

With my O levels satisfactorily negotiated before we left Sussex, A levels were the next hurdle set before me, but not before I had had a discussion with my father about what I intended to do as a career.

Occasionally my mother visited the hairdresser, and given my limited knowledge of career choices this seemed to me an ideal occupation, in which I could combine my desire to help people with my need to create and use my hands, and which importantly I felt would be within my capabilities.

The tentative suggestion of hairdressing as a future career for the daughter for whom he had such grand ambitions was met with a long silence from my father, a stony and somewhat irritated gaze, and then the carefully chosen words, 'There are two professions: medicine and law. You are hopeless at mathematics so you had better study law.'

My heart sank but I knew rebellion would be futile and so the die was cast. He had overlooked accounts and revenue, both important elements of a legal training, but even if I had known that then it would have been useless as his mind was made up. My A levels were duly chosen and I was enrolled into the local technical college for the next phase of my life and education.

I enjoyed my days at the college, working hard and making

friends easily. The world was beginning to open up for me, which my parents somewhat begrudgingly accepted provided my academic progress was not compromised as a result. Being reasonably presentable, with very long thick hair, I caught the eye of the art and photography department and whenever possible I would pop in, to be greeted with that easy welcome so unique to art students. These visits made a refreshing change from the world of academia, promising the possibility of a realm hitherto unknown to me – that of the arts in general.

The art department prevailed upon me to take part in a rag week procession as Lady Godiva, seated in a horse-drawn carriage with everything very tastefully arranged and my long hair being strategically positioned to cover any embarrassment. Little did I know that a picture of Lady Godiva was to grace the front page of the local newspaper...

At breakfast on the following Saturday morning my father carefully folded the paper he had been reading with the front page uppermost, laid it in front of me and asked with a face like thunder, 'Am I to assume that Lady Godiva and my daughter are one and the same?'

Although totally taken aback, I mustered all the confidence I had begun to acquire and in as calm a voice as I could manage suggested that he had probably got up to far worse as a medical student. To my relief and amazement he accepted the challenge in good part and no more was said.

Sadly, the approach of yet more examinations meant my visits to the art department became all too infrequent and enquiries were already underway to find a firm of solicitors with whom I could take articles.

At around this time, my parents finally settled on the purchase of a house and we moved again, by this time getting quite used to the process.

It was at our new house that I again had reason to be thankful for my parents' chosen calling. The house had extensive lawned areas, and as part of the long established tradition of sharing chores it fell to me to be responsible for their upkeep, partly because my father's health had never been that robust and my mother was too busy with other matters. It took a full four to five hours to complete the mowing and trimming.

On one particular occasion it had rained the previous day, so the back of the rotary machine had become clogged with wet grass. Hot, tired and not thinking straight, I attempted to clear the blockage forgetting to stop the motor. Fortunately, the blades were not too sharp but the force alone was enough to badly crush the tops of two fingers, the action of the blades leaving them only partially attached. My hand looked an awful mess, with impacted mud and grass and blood beginning to seep through. Presumably through shock, I felt no pain at this stage: just panic about how I was to tell my parents how stupid I had been.

With my hand behind my back I entered the kitchen where they were sitting and said rather apologetically, 'I'm sorry, Dad, I've had an accident with the machine,' to which he rather curtly replied, 'I trust you haven't damaged it.'

Needless to say, as I brought my hand into view his demeanour completely changed. As I have mentioned before, in a genuine emergency their care could not have been better. Quickly, my father assembled what he needed, with my mother's help, and for what seemed an eternity he bathed, cleaned, tidied, trimmed, reassembled, repositioned and stitched, finally strapping and bandaging my hand. To begin with I didn't feel too much pain, and his efforts fascinated me; but by the time he had finished my hand was hurting badly and I was also distressed to see that he was as white as a sheet.

As soon as he finished he left, and we heard him being violently sick in the downstairs toilet. He told me later that knowing what had to be done and that to have a chance of success it had to be done quickly, and as in any emergency situation he got on with the task. The ensuing nausea was solely due his being aware that he was having to work without anaesthesia thereby causing his own daughter considerable pain, albeit in a good cause.

All I can say is that due to his quick thinking and skill I still have a full quota of fingers and no one would ever know how close I came to losing two valuable digits.

The necessary A levels were achieved, I was accepted by the Law Society, articles were entered into with a local firm of solicitors and the daunting prospect of five years' training with yet more examinations stretched before me.

A Defining Moment

As an articled clerk my weekly salary was thirty shillings (£1.50) per week, and from the outset I was made aware that this level of remuneration should be viewed as generous. In earlier times, solicitors were entitled to exact a premium from the family of an articled clerk as payment for the training to be provided, and therefore I should consider myself lucky to be paid at all. Although even by the standards of the time the pay was low, as I was living at home and had never been accustomed to having money of my own I felt no particular resentment. However, a vital element in the reasoning I was given was the quality of the training to be provided. Here, being female proved to be a handicap, as immediately my role was perceived as a useful mix of tea lady, receptionist, telephonist, filer and general factotem – with some legal instruction thrown in when convenient.

No formal or legislative constraints relating to sexual equality or sex discrimination existed then, and thus rather than gaining any legal experience I acquired a good working knowledge of general office procedure, including of course tea making. In addition, the ritual bottom-pinching by the senior partner when presented with his tea was rather tiresome – no laws against sexual harassment then either!

I worked hard at this bewildering variety of tasks, picking up as much of the law as I was able, and gradually, particularly with the first professional examinations approaching, I managed to become more involved in the work for which I had joined the firm.

The practice had no particular speciality so I gained some knowledge and grounding in the procedural aspects of probate, conveyancing and matrimonial law, and it was in connection with the last of these that quite unexpectedly my life was to change.

In connection with the more complex or contentious matrimonial cases, counsel would be briefed, and conferences with counsel, client and solicitor would ensue followed in due course by a hearing in court. As part of my training, I occasionally accompanied my principal to these conferences and hearings in London and in time attended on my own, particularly when I had been conducting the case myself and was therefore fully conversant with the facts and had gained the confidence of the client.

Groups of barristers tend to work from particular chambers and solicitors generally favour certain chambers a good understanding and working relationship resulting between the two.

Increasingly my work centred around matrimonial cases and because of this I frequently visited chambers, the members and clerks of which were extremely kind to me. One up-and-coming barrister was particularly helpful and supportive. Although undoubtedly aware of my limited knowledge, after delivering an erudite opinion to the client he would often turn to me and ask if I concurred. With this sort of encouragement and boost to my confidence, learning became more enjoyable and worthwhile.

Over the months it became clear that the easy and comfortable empathy between us extended beyond the law and we would find time to be together whenever the opportunity arose around hearings or conferences. However, such extended meetings were necessarily discreet, the stumbling block to this otherwise romantic tale being of course that the young man in question was married...

We were both acutely aware that our growing attachment was wrong, and yet somehow, as so often happens, those standards vehemently held in youth seemed to waver, and hitherto unacknowledged areas of grey began to confuse the distinctions between black and white. The relationship continued and my barrister friend was adamant his marriage had been a mistake. It was now a marriage in name only, and that when the time was right he would leave and we would be together. It sounds so trite now but in my naivety I believed him, and even after so long I think he genuinely intended a future for us.

I was required to be absent from the office for nine months' college attendance preparatory to my first professional examinations. Part of me feared while another almost hoped that this interruption in our routine would resolve matters, but both to my delight and dismay the little car I knew so well by then would appear as if by magic, waiting for me in the college drive. I once read that the greatest romances are those that are never consummated, and when I look back at the hours we talked and the intensity of the feeling that existed between us and remind myself that adultery was never committed, I can readily relate to that sentiment, so just maybe not all my core values had been forgotten.

We settled into an almost surreal routine with a patience born of hope and love. I felt as though my life was taking shape with a definite future towards which I could work, and even the relentless burden of study became less onerous. My parents met him and approved, seeming to overlook his marital status and accepting as I did that all would be settled one day without anyone being hurt. In effect his marriage was over – the ease and frequency of our meetings seeming to reinforce this belief.

The college course was punctuated by frequent tests and evaluations of our progress, on completion of which it became traditional for a few of us to celebrate at the local hostelry. My fellow students were aware that I had a close friend but other than that details were not discussed.

Following one of these tests, which had been particularly trying for us all, we decided to push the boat out and go into town for a celebratory lunch. Laughing and chatting as we approached the public house one of my friends pushed open the door to usher me in first.

It took only a moment for me to absorb the scene that met my eyes but that defining moment altered the whole course of my life. Standing a few feet before me was the man who had made himself the centre of my world and upon whom all my hopes and dreams for the future depended. In a fleeting moment that fantasy collapsed, for standing happily by his side was his wife – his very obviously pregnant wife.

In those few seconds I grew up, learning my first harsh lesson of betrayal. I continued standing unable to move and the friends who had followed me in began to realise something was wrong and gathered round. Their attention thus drawn the couple at the bar turned; the sight of their faces broke my trance and I turned and ran. A couple of my fellow students, alarmed by my unusual behaviour, came after me. Somehow I managed to compose myself enough to offer a feeble excuse of suddenly feeling unwell, thanked them for their concern and said I would be all right by the next day.

Left alone, I walked for hours; to this day I have no recollection exactly where I went or for how long. Even now it is difficult to describe the gamut of emotions through which I travelled. Strangely, I remember feeling no anger, just an enormous void where my dreams had been. Amazingly, I also had sympathy in my heart for his feelings, for whatever wrong he had done I had no doubt of the feeling that existed between us. However, despite wishing I could find some alternative explanation for what I had seen, I knew there was none and that this fact must signal the end of something so vital to me that to continue without it seemed impossible.

I turned all this over and over in my mind but eventually the practical side of my nature began to surface and, finding myself sitting on a bench by the river staring at the water, I realised I had to pull myself together, as in some ways the nightmare was far from over. I knew him well enough to know that he would try to find a way to continue with our plans and that I would have ultimately to face him and deal with that confrontation.

The immediate future presented me with the problem of not arousing suspicion in those around me that anything was amiss. I had confided my relationship to none except my parents, and I certainly would neither seek nor expect consolation there. Devoid of any feeling or plan other than a determination to appear as normal as possible and so buy time until I felt better, I returned home. I was told there had been several telephone calls for me, but on the pretext of feeling a bit under the weather I made my excuses and retired to my room. I expect by this time I looked every bit as drained as I felt so my explanation was easily accepted. Although not aware of exactly what had occurred I suspect my parents guessed more than I imagined, for the young man's name was never ever mentioned again.

I needed the next few days to think, settle down and decide in my own mind how to cope with a meeting which I knew would be inevitable and indeed necessary. Having in those few days ignored innumerable messages via the college and office to make contact, I then received a letter pleading for a meeting in London, and by this time I knew that I was as ready as I would ever be to say goodbye.

Our meeting was probably the first of several occasions in my life when knowing exactly what I had to do offered no comfort. As we sat by the Embankment I listened to him tell me how the pregnancy was not the result of a loving relationship, together with empassioned pleas for another chance to sort everything out so that we could really start our future together. It was an impressive performance and he used his skills as a barrister to the full but he said nothing that I had not anticipated, and I had already decided that whereas I had been prepared to step between two parties locked in a loveless marriage, no way would I do so where a child was involved.

When his efforts at persuasion had subsided I told him quietly what I had decided and why. There was a silence and my heart went out to him seeing the desperation and agony in his face and realising that his distress was as much if not more than my own. I had felt no anger towards him but even if I had done so in that moment I would have forgiven all. As he promised his love for me could not be denied and that he would still find a way, I repeated that despite my love for him there was no way. With this I rose rather unsteadily, announcing my intention to catch the train home, and we walked in silence hand in hand over Waterloo Bridge. Halfway across I stopped and turned, tears burning my eyes, kissed him and in a barely audible whisper said my final goodbye.

Pulling myself from his embrace I again fled, not looking back despite the despairing calls to change my mind that followed me. I made my way straight to the station for I knew that if I delayed the temptation to turn back and find him would be irresistible. It seemed as though every fibre of my being was pulling me back to where I wanted to be more than anything else in the world, but the still small voice of reason and sanity prevailed.

Fortunately the train I caught was a slow one giving me ample time yet again to try and disentangle my emotions and formulate some strategy to deal with the mess that up until a few days ago had been my life. I longed to be back with him, comfort him and share again everything we had come to expect and enjoy, but that time had gone and somehow I must now concentrate on a different future without him.

For the first part of the journey I just sat looking blankly at the seat opposite me. As it was by now late in the evening I had few fellow travellers to interfere with my thoughts and slowly I began to think more pragmatically. Although the anguish of my situation seemed unique to me most certainly I was not the first to be caught in this way and undoubtedly would not be the last. Therefore, was I prepared to let this period in my life – however difficult – blight the rest? That seemed to be punishing myself again for a very hard lesson already learnt. However, with all the common sense I was endeavouring to muster, there was one fact I knew could never alter – never again would I feel for anyone as I did for the man from whom I had just parted.

As the train and my thoughts travelled on I wondered if marriage and children could be part of my future now. While I was convinced the depth of feeling I had experienced could never be repeated, surely such intense affection was not always essential for a marriage to be successful. Many partnerships thrived on joint endeavour and friendship, and in some cases love would ensue. Provided that I gave all I could in terms of affection, hard work and commitment to someone, the absence of what I knew to be impossible for me need not adversely affect the long term happiness of such an arrangement.

So it was on a train late one evening that I made a secret pact with myself. I had been lucky enough to have experienced a love possibly denied to others, the story of which was my own; but now I had to move on. If my destiny should decree that I met someone with no particular emotional demands but who would welcome affection, hard work, children and a complete commitment to do all possible to ensure a happy relationship, then I would be ready, willing and able to make such a marriage.

Alighting from the train, I made my way home so exhausted I could hardly walk. Feeling utterly alone and as though my heart would break under the strain, even the conviction that I had made the right decision did nothing to lessen the pain.

By now it was very late and I let myself into the house, relieved to find no one waiting up for me. Not bothering to undress I stretched out on my bed, grateful for a chance to rest at last. At least I had somehow negotiated what would surely come to rank as the hardest day of my life. Little did I know then that years later in quite different circumstances and for very different reasons I would again feel a sense of utter desolation and despair. I would learn a deeper sadness fraught with feelings of guilt, shame and failure, for which I endlessly sought resolution but from which there seemed no escape.

As for now, however, whatever the cause of my present torment it was not the result of deliberate malice or unkindness inflicted by one person upon another.

Reaching for my faithful companion and trustee of all my thoughts, I closed my eyes, and with Edward held tightly in my arms surrendered to perhaps the greatest healer of all – sleep.

The Journey Continues

As my faithful reader will readily imagine, the days ahead were not easy. With examinations imminent I threw myself into study, it being really the only other world I knew. By immersing myself so completely in the one, I hoped to avoid thought of the other as much as possible. I tried my utmost to show no outward signs of the recent upheaval in my life and thankfully my efforts were rewarded. No one appeared to notice any change in me, attributing my more than usual attention to study to the approach of examinations.

Perhaps owing to the happy frame of mind surrounding my earlier studies or the intense work I did immediately prior to the exams, or more probably a combination of both, to my complete amazement and the delight of my ever ambitious parents I passed all the examinations with distinction.

This first part of my training completed, I returned to the office to be awarded a pay rise of ten shillings (50p) taking my weekly salary to the giddy heights of £2!

Although this was by no means the main reason, it was one of several factors which decided me to transfer my articles to another firm. The main reason was that a physical move away from my previous firm, and in particular the branch of law with which I had become so involved, was obviously sensible.

In addition my parents had decided to move away from the immediate area with a view to their eventual retirement. As there was no easy means of transport between their intended property and the town where my firm and college were located, it was clear that I would have to find accommodation of my own, which would clearly be impossible on £2 per week.

Fortunately, during my initial grounding in general office procedure I had acquired passable typing skills, and together with primitive shorthand helped by an extremely reliable memory, I secured as position as a secretary to a solicitor to whom my articles were transferred. Despite my weekly salary rising to the princely sum of £18 per week, life was far from luxurious in a tiny flat with rent, rates, heating and food to pay for, but I managed.

The interval between the two periods of obligatory college attendance was quite short and of course, as my salary from the office would cease during such absence, my ability to sustain myself and so complete my professional training depended on whether any grant I might obtain would be sufficient to fund me through that time. I had received a grant in respect of the first examinations but that had been understandably small as I had been living at home.

The response to the next application was to say the least disappointing. Despite my success with the initial examinations I was told that as I had not attained the age of twenty-five the major part of any funding was still the responsibility of my parents. I disputed this, particularly as I had been living completely independently from them financially for well over a year. The authority concerned nevertheless insisted that my parents' salaries must be taken into account in calculating the amount of any grant, and the only way this could be avoided was for my father to swear on affidavit to the Minister of Education that he refused to support his daughter.

I flatly refused to put my father through such an ordeal, partly on principle, as I could see neither merit nor relevance in the arbitrary rulings in relation to my age or my parents' financial circumstances. However, the main reason for my refusal was my father's failing health, and that having not worked for several months it was unlikely he would do so again. This situation had arisen from an unfortunate sequence of events for my parents, and I had no intention of adding to their worries.

I mentioned at the beginning of this narrative that my mother had had five confinements. The first of these produced twin boys who sadly died shortly after birth, and she was left critically ill, eventually needing several blood transfusions. Probably because of the pressures of wartime, the blood so given was slightly contaminated, causing her to develop a bizarre and unpredictable allergy. Although thankfully this manifested itself infrequently, when it did the results were both dramatic and alarming. Areas of her body – usually her arms, hands, shoulders or face – would suddenly erupt into enormous swellings. As these episodes were infrequent they presented more of a nuisance than a danger, and because copious administration of antihistamine helped the swellings disperse, no intense investigation as to cause or remedy had been undertaken.

That was to change following the incident which so unsettled them after their move. At this time they were still working as Medical Officers for the Army, and brought to those posts their usual level of dedication and reliability. I can only ever recall three instances where either of them excused themselves from work on grounds of ill health. The first two related to my father who, when in general practice in Essex, had worked himself literally almost to death. Firstly he ignored pneumonia, which as a former tuberculosis sufferer was doubly dangerous for him, and secondly he eventually collapsed with a burst appendix.

The third absence involved my mother and resulted in an absurd chain of events immensely upsetting for them both. My mother had awoken with one of these allergy-related swellings in her neck which rapidly assumed alarming proportions. My father telephoned both their places of work, explaining that neither would be reporting for duty but that he would keep them apprised of developments.

The swelling had begun to compromise my mother's airway and the prospect of emergency surgery in the shape of a tracheotomy loomed large. Thankfully, however, with the assistance of their local doctor, the need for such drastic action was narrowly averted and the crisis passed. The whole episode had left my mother so weak and my father so exhausted that sensibly it was decided neither of them should return to work until the following week. They were both surprised and touched by flowers and messages of understanding and encouragement received from their colleagues.

It was therefore a complete shock that on the morning of their return to work my mother received a letter from the Ministry terminating her employment on the grounds of her absence through ill health.

Although obviously the result of some ridiculous bureaucratic mix-up, it upset my mother and my father lost his temper. He rarely did this, and the only other occasion I can recall him being so angry was on checking my mother's car after she had collected it from a service he had found that every wheel nut was barely finger-tight. The ensuing telephone conversation must have left the garage in no doubt that not only had they lost my father's patronage but that they were lucky to have avoided proceedings against them for negligence.

On this occasion he telephoned the Ministry telling them in no uncertain terms that if this was an example of how they treated their personnel then not only would my mother no longer be working for them, neither would he, and he resigned.

Needless to say, abject apologies from high-ranking officials quickly followed, endeavouring to put matters right, and to a degree they succeeded. My mother was assured her position was and always had been secure and my father's resignation would be ignored.

Always a proud and somewhat stubborn man, my father decided to stand his ground, refusing to withdraw his resignation. I think with retirement not far ahead and the recent upset having done nothing to help his already indifferent health, he just felt too tired to continue. The extreme nature of my mother's latest allergic reaction did at least prompt investigation into the cause, and following a long and painful course of desensitisation injections the problem was eventually solved.

So it was that whereas my mother returned to work, my father never worked again and I resolved I would not involve them in a battle with the education authority over my funding.

I had actually started my course before the authority deemed fit to tell me the amount of my grant. My fees were to be paid, together with a sum just under £50, on which I was apparently expected to exist for six months. It was madness to even have contemplated it, but having started at the college I determined to try.

Like many people of my generation I have an abhorrence of debt, having grown up with the principle that nothing should be acquired unless sufficient funds are available. Therefore, particularly with winter almost upon me, I had an impossible task ahead.

Payments of rent and rates were essential and made inroads into the little I had been able to save. Practicalities such as food and keeping warm, although equally important for my survival, had necessarily to be kept as low in cost as possible.

I developed various strategies to deal with my impecunious circumstances. I walked the quite long distance to and from college, making as much use of the warm library as I could for study. On a Friday I would return earlier via the town's market and purchase my provisions for the week, usually comprising bread, cheese and a cauliflower. This together with milk which was delivered and the very few extras I could afford from a little store next to the flats would have to last the week. I well remember my dismay at once finding the centre of a cauliflower rotten and useless and counting up coins to see what, if anything, I could afford from the store to bridge the gap.

I had few clothes and no way of drying them except by allowing them to drip until dry enough for me to wear in order to complete the drying process. I lived in a tiny flat and kept the heat as low as possible, and Edward and I would frequently retire early to bed with my legal books and the bed piled high with dry clothes in an effort to keep warm and progress my studies before going to sleep.

Looking back, although admittedly it was a very difficult time, I have no regrets, as it served to reinforce my ability to cope in the face of adversity both mentally as well as physically. I have never had leanings towards extravagance but if I had, living as I did then provided a salutary lesson in appreciating values, despising waste and making do – qualities that I am sure were tested to the full during wartime.

Despite my best efforts, studying within an atmosphere of rising debt and the inevitable effects of being chronically cold and hungry took their toll. I knew I could not continue.

Just before Christmas I wrote to the college informing them of my decision to abandon my training even at this late hour. They accepted that without adequate funding, over which they had no control, it was impossible for me to carry on, and with regret they accepted my resignation.

The prospect of telling my parents filled me with dread. As

well as the overwhelming sense of disappointment I knew they would feel at my apparent failure to fulfil the high ambitions they had always held for me, I was also filled with apprehension at upsetting them at all. Now that their involvement with the medical world was drawing to a close, they had become almost reclusive and the enduring distance between my father and my brother seemed more and more to depress and sadden him. My parents had settled into a routine in which they seemed to manage, and the last thing I wanted to do with disrupt this more than necessary.

Therefore, before telling them about giving up my course, I had made enquiries and discovered that although I would now cancel my articles, the qualifications I had achieved to date could be used towards a lesser but still valuable qualification in the law, and one for which I could complete the necessary work by correspondence course and continued employment within a legal firm.

My news was greeted with quiet resignation and obvious disappointment, only slightly ameliorated by the alternative plan I had decided to pursue. It was as though having failed to reach the very top of my profession any different direction my career might take warranted no further interest, and was eclipsed by small day to day events which were occurring in my parents' increasingly small world. In some ways I was hurt by this attitude, after having worked so hard to please them rather than to realise any ambitions of my own. On the other hand, it was also an immense relief to have the enormous burden of expectation which had weighed so heavily for many years largely lifted. In fact, they took little further interest in my work at all, showing marked indifference when eventually I obtained a Fellowship, which represented at least some recognised written qualification of some standing for which they had apparently yearned so much.

After breaking the news of my change of course I returned to the office in the hope of working on there after cancellation of my articles, studying from home via the correspondence course and building up the necessary length of service within a legal firm. Unfortunately for some inexplicable reason my principal saw my change in status from articled clerk to 'legal secretary' as grounds to mix pleasure with business – a view which I did not share – and so again I was forced to change to another firm of solicitors. Fortunately, with no articles to be transferred it was merely a case of finding a new employer, and with now really quite wide experience this did not present too much difficulty for me.

By the time the required eight years within a legal environment was completed, I had moved firms again and was fortunate to be working for a very large firm of solicitors who were kind enough to acknowledge the range of abilities I had acquired and used them all. I was a secretary to a partner, where I could use not just my legal knowledge but also my practical abilities to deal with personnel and office equipment and generally keep things running smoothly.

They were extremely generous financially and more importantly gave me a feeling of self-esteem, worth and confidence hitherto unknown to me, for which I was and still am very grateful.

When I made the decision to leave, for reasons which will become clear later, although aware of my dilemma they made it clear that they wanted me to stay, and indeed expressed the view that it would better for me to do so. They suggested a year's sabbatical with my job being held open for me, but rightly or wrongly I felt such an arrangement would leave them and me in an unfair state of limbo, and so albeit with great sadness I left. It is a pointless exercise now to speculate how a different decision would have affected my future. Dwelling on what might have been rarely helps.

It was the difficulties and problems arising from the ill health of the man I had married a few years before that had prompted my leaving, and that relationship will be the subject of the rest of this narrative. It will be the most difficult part to write, representing as it does a period spanning over half my life at the time of writing – a time filled with unhappiness, disappointment and constant self-doubt, and an endless challenge to my resolve to make any marriage into which I entered a success.

The thought of so many years of struggle and heartache amounting to nothing more than a waste of time troubles me greatly.

By sharing through this book not only the feelings of fear and wretched despair experienced over that time, but also the knowledge that eventual freedom and relative safety can be secured, I have sought to give hope to others similarly afflicted.

In my narrative to date I have endeavoured to provide the background and in some respects an explanation for what follows, and the efforts I made to adapt and deal with a life and relationship so different from that for which I had hoped and worked so hard. I am by no means without fault myself, but at least my conscience is clear in that over all those sad years I did by best.

For Better or for Worse

As I said at the end of the previous chapter, the experiences which prompted me to write this book spanned over half my life at the time of writing. However, as I intend to live to a ripe old age despite somewhat indifferent health, hopefully those years that were so unhappy will ultimately form but a small portion of an otherwise normal existence, albeit one filled with the usual ups and downs.

As I write, it is three years since I took what was for me the momentous decision to admit defeat and cease trying to breathe life into a marriage that had never really existed. No one party is ever blameless in the breakdown of a relationship and I have never claimed to be without fault. However, my conscience is clear that I held true to the bargain I made with myself years earlier and to the vows I made on my wedding day. I ceaselessly adapted my life to fit in with my husband's needs and demands, only to be met with coldness and latterly abuse.

Three years ago I could not have written this book being as I was totally consumed with the guilt of perceived failure, the misery of humiliation and overwhelming fatigue resulting from years of fear and uncertainty. The desire to help through sharing has been with me for years, but the time had to be right for me to be as fair as I am able in telling my story. Now, three years on and in my sixty-second year, that time has come to complete the task I set myself.

I have no desire to be vindictive in what follows; I see no point in revenge any more than I see the purpose in cruelty or violence. However, enough of the truth must be told for the narrative to serve its overall purpose. There are some things I will never tell, such is the sense of shame that unjustly lingers for having allowed them to happen, and sadly I am certain there are countless others who bear similar emotional scars.

With the intention therefore of being fair and factual, I will embark upon the narrative of my 'marriage'. If any persons mentioned in the ensuing pages object to what I have written then they must look to their own consciences, as I have been entirely honest and truthful and indeed in many instances have erred on the side of understatement. My overwhelming desire is to help those who find themselves in similar circumstances, not to punish or offend those involved in my own misery, and I must leave it up to the reader to judge if I have been true to that aim.

While visiting my parents one weekend a neighbour enlisted my help to accompany their daughter on what they thought was a somewhat dubious date, on the basis that the gentleman would bring his friend thereby making up a foursome. So it was that I embarked on the only blind date of my life although as far as I was concerned it was merely to keep a diplomatic eye on things as requested. My companion seemed pleasant as did his friend and the evening passed well enough.

It transpired that my companion's home was not far from my little flat, and although the relationship between his friend and the young lady did not proceed he made it clear he would like to see me again. To describe the ensuing months as a courtship would be an exaggeration. We both had demanding jobs and I was still studying and very short of money. We had days out and he would sometimes come to the flat in the evening, always hungry, despite having apparently eaten 'a meal' at home. I was puzzled by his unusual reserve and quietness until I met his immediate family, who I think I can fairly say were untypical in their relationships with each other as well as their attitude to outsiders.

Outside his immediate family I was welcomed with respect and kindness and still am to this day from those still surviving. His immediate family however were very different. His sister made her dislike of me clear from the start; it later came to light that in her eyes I presented a threat to her father's affection for her. His mother droned on endlessly about neighbourhood gossip and the virtues of my friend's previous girlfriend, while his father tried to be as polite as he could without causing friction with his wife and daughter. I learnt much more later from him and other members of the family, but at the time it all seemed rather strange to me, and I felt sorry for their son almost in a way that I had done for the injured birds I had rescued as a child. I felt that the curious lack of emotion and unusual reserve must be symptomatic of a strangely inhibited background and upbringing.

Even with the benefit of hindsight I cannot say how much of what followed was due to upbringing or just the uniqueness of everyone as an individual. As I said at the beginning of this book, and still firmly believe, we are all given a life and it is up to each and every one of us to use it to the best of our abilities. Inevitably some have a more difficult start in life than others and many are stricken by illness or disability, but I do not believe that either of these circumstances must necessarily result in such a level of resentment and bitterness as to justify unkindness to others. Conversely, there seem to be many examples of courage overcoming disadvantage and providing shining beacons of hope and comfort.

The months went by and, as I imagine often happens, the relationship drifted into marriage. I was quite relieved to have had no great emotional or physical demands made on me, and believed that in time in a committed relationship of love and understanding his restraint and reserve would ease, and what seemed a good working relationship would prosper and deepen. Then, with children and all the joy they can bring, the marriage would be a success. I wonder how many mothers have told their daughters never to enter into marriage thinking that a man can be changed. In fact, my mother never advised me thus, and I found out for myself all too soon anyway.

Looking back, most would have been dazzled by the plethora of warning lights that I ignored, so blinkered was I in my determination to make everything a success. According to his mother my engagement ring was quite wrong; and then, in the hearing and to the astonishment of my employer, she was extraordinarily rude to me over the telephone, which my fiancé steadfastly refused to challenge. The wedding invitation sent by my parents was acknowledged by an offensive refusal and understandably they were becoming increasingly alarmed about how events were developing. My father's health in particular was deteriorating, and I shied away from upsetting or involving my parents more than necessary. They tolerated my fiancé but their attitude was tempered by their concern over my treatment by his family and his lack of support for me. My mother grudgingly came with me to choose my dress; neither my in-laws nor my husband showed the slightest interest or enthusiasm at all.

I wish to avoid turning any part of this narrative into a litany of woes or a catalogue of misdemeanours, and I am sure I have mentioned enough for my reader to grasp the general picture.

My wedding day was very far from the happiest day of my life. At the eleventh hour his parents – though not sister – decided they would come to the church, but not the reception, and during the photograph taking after the ceremony I was completely ignored. As we drove away at the end of that dismal day it began to rain; I little knew then that it would be nearly forty years before the storm clouds would finally clear away.

The evening of our wedding night was subdued and I put this down to the nervous strain of a long and tiring day overshadowed by the bickering within his family. Apart from the praise of friends I had received no compliments regarding my appearance, dress or flowers, and it was as though the end of a rather tiresome business meeting was being welcomed with a quiet sense of relief. However, I determined to put any feelings of disappointment behind me and look forward. I had attributed a lack of passionate advances prior to our marriage to gentlemanly respect, and with my accustomed optimism assumed that in the fullness of time the intimacy of a normal healthy marriage would resolve any problems arising from my fiancé's apparent natural reserve. Yet again I was to be disillusioned, as it became all too clear that intimacy would not be part of our relationship. The initial lovemaking was awkward, but again I put this down to fatigue and stress. On waking after a few hours' sleep, I cuddled up to my new husband, who woke and demanded to know why I should need to 'do it again' as we had already 'done it once'…

The cold hand of panic and dismay which had been slowly stealing around my heart all day finally won. My husband quickly returned to sleep, uncaring or oblivious to anything amiss. I rose and sat by the window and tried to come to terms with the realisation that in all probability I had made an awful mistake. What had I done? Yes, I had resigned myself to a lack of grand passion but this – no passion at all? Would it ever come, or had I really condemned myself to a life with no love? Was this the punishment I had earned for making that pact with myself and for making wedding vows with only future love in mind – was this all my fault? Night turned to dawn and then to day. Although mentally and physically exhausted I knew it was too late to turn back. I had to carry on – I had to make things work and believe I could succeed. What was the alternative? I could not see one. Sadly, I was to learn all too soon that sex to my husband was something in which he indulged when he wanted, on his terms, and with complete disregard for my feelings.

Either through boredom or finding satisfaction in other ways, his sexual demands became less frequent. For this I was grateful, as such occasions were humiliating, painful and totally lacking in love at any level.

When he wakened on our wedding morning he assumed I was already up and dressed because I was frightened of the flight ahead of us. I did not disillusion him and afterwards he frequently joked to friends that I had been so nervous about my first flight that I had got up during my wedding night... Little did they know the real reason.

The honeymoon passed well enough – a welcome break from work and all the tension that had existed before the wedding – but there was no passion, no excitement or intimacy, and therefore it was with a sense of relief as well as sadness that I returned to the flat I had secured for us from a client and began my married life in earnest, still struggling to honour my resolve that somehow I could make our marriage a success.

Despite all my best efforts, any attempt to introduce affection or love into the physical side of our relationship failed miserably and on one occasion resulted in me being struck by my husband. Very calmly I told him that if the violence was ever repeated I would leave. I resigned myself that intercourse was something to be endured when he demanded it and I must do as bidden – to be still and silent and nothing more. Strangely, many years later when the violence erupted again, I think it was that more than anything else that confirmed my decision to end the marriage.

However, for the time being my warning was heeded and our

marriage continued on the predictable lines of working hard and saving for a home of our own. We both worked long hours but it became quickly apparent that although I worked as long, if not longer, hours, the responsibility for the physical chores of running a home – shopping, cooking, housework, washing, ironing, gardening, window cleaning etc. – was mine and mine alone.

In fairness, I came into marriage at the tail end of an era when men were waited on by their women, when women did not also go out to work all day, and before modern man came into being, turning his hands to many domestic duties previously considered inappropriate. Also, unknown to either of us at the time, my husband may have been suffering the early stages of the illness which was sadly to afflict him later. However, taking all that into account, I vividly remember comments made by neighbours and friends asking why he didn't get his act together and help. Somehow it all seemed to be part of the lack of togetherness which permeated every aspect of our relationship.

Contact with his immediate family was infrequent, and owing to their continued hostility to me I saw very little of them at all, for which I was thankful. Other members of his family welcomed me warmly and even expressed to me their concern at the lack of affection I was being shown by my husband. Through a mixture of misplaced loyalty and a stubborn refusal to accept failure, I covered for him, making excuses about tiredness or shyness; but as with all untruths once begun they persist and ever so slowly the trap tightens and the isolation deepens.

My parents accepted my husband with politeness, being streetwise enough to realise that if they did not it would be difficult for me to visit. Their own health was not good and as usual they were preoccupied with their own concerns and much as I loved them I knew not to look in their direction for sympathy or advice. I am sure they knew I was unhappy but it was not in their natures to reach out and comfort. In many ways I am glad they did not realise the extent of my unhappiness, although I know towards the end of my mother's life when she relied on me for help, she guessed some although by no means all of that sadness.

Just a few years into our marriage, on the eve of visiting some friends, my husband was taken ill at work and was found to have a slight defect in his heart rhythm. This involved a certain amount of treatment, all of which was very successful, and with appropriate medication it caused him no further trouble, although from then on he was even more careful and selective about what activities he felt he could manage.

We had moved again to a larger house, and with his health stable I floated the idea of children. I think I knew it was the last throw of the dice to make a successful marriage and maybe awaken a part of him that I had been unable to reach. My problem was conception and because of the complete lack of intimacy between us there ensued unpleasant arguments about when intercourse could 'be arranged'. Quite remarkably, I managed to become pregnant on a few occasions but sadly none went to full term, and eventually the consultant (who I think had guessed some measure of my torment) suggested I should stop. At no time would my husband attend clinics, scans or appointments with the consultant, and again I was left feeling humiliated, isolated and with that ever present feeling of failure. After my last miscarriage the consultant requested my husband to attend, which he did, but he refused to see the consultant and it was on that occasion the consultant suggested very gently that we should stop. It was the right decision for so many reasons, and all things considered, although I longed for children to have brought a child into such a relationship in such a contrived manner would have bordered on the obscene.

That feeling of entrapment which was to reach epic proportions later was beginning to grow. What could I do? Should I keep trying to make this work at some level or should I admit defeat? I had worked in matrimonial law – I knew not all marriages worked – but what about my promises both to myself and on my wedding day? Surely, there must be a compromise – somewhere, somehow. I tried so hard to forgive my husband's reluctance to love me and to care, and tried to keep our relationship on some sort of even keel.

I was very fortunate in having some friends we had made through his work who had two little girls. Their mother and I became very close friends and I adored the girls. The families would get together most weeks, and without the understanding and comfort of that friendship life at that stage would have been far more difficult for me. She too had her problems and we shared our worries and supported each other enormously, greatly lessening our respective feelings of isolation.

My husband became even more moody and declared he was depressed – for which as usual I was to blame. By now, I had come to accept that if anything went wrong, somehow or other it would be my fault however illogical the chain of causation might be – that is one of the ways the trap steadily tightens without you even being aware. However, I insisted we seek medical advice, which resulted in a diagnosis of a degenerative disease. Having a good grounding in medicine I knew fairly well what this meant and, given my husband's character, I abandoned any further hope of children or a normal marriage and felt that any thought of leaving was out of the question, knowing he would need considerable help and support in the future. We were lucky enough to have a brilliant and understanding consultant who combined compassion with firmness and to whom I will always be grateful for the kindness he showed to us both and the support he gave me.

So my life changed again. I made the decision to abandon my career, take part-time work so I was better able to keep everything together at home, still contribute financially but also be available to make leisure hours as happy and stress-free for my husband as possible. I had long given up any hope of having a loving marriage but I still clung to the hope of a compromise where we could be friends and work together to give him the support he needed in a warm, pleasant environment surrounded by our friends, enjoying life as much as possible, and I would have the flexibility to adapt and modify my life as needed to meet his increasing demands. That was my intention, but despite my best efforts and endeavours it did not work out that way. I know so well with hindsight that such a plan could only have worked had it been based on the one thing that had never existed – a close and loving marriage.

For Worse

If I found the last chapter difficult to write, the next two promised to be the hardest of all. They conclude with the culmination of all the unkindness and rejection, in response to which I finally found the courage to turn and walk away. Yes, I left with a feeling of utter despair, isolation and failure, but strangely I also had a sense of complete certainty and calm.

For the time being, however, I accepted my role as carer with no particular feelings either way. Looking back, I think even then I had begun to discipline myself not to feel anything because of the pain it caused. I learnt to forget who I was and just cope with each day as it came in the hope that somehow I could deal with the next. We enjoyed a reasonable standard of living in a nice house in a pleasant village, and so I thought I had much to be grateful for and the means with which to face a relatively secure future.

Sadly, the friends to whom we had grown close were struck by a double tragedy. The husband was diagnosed with leukaemia, which exacerbated an existing condition of psoriasis in his wife. Both very pragmatic people, they realised the outlook for neither of them was good and sensibly made adequate provision for their daughters, who by this time had left home and were beginning lives of their own. However, it was a desperately difficult time for the whole family and we did what we could to help. Sadly they died within a year of each other, and while in no way have I ever aspired to take their mother's place, I have tried over the years to be available for the children if needed, as their parents had requested me to do. Both are now married with families of their own, and the younger daughter in particular is as close to me as if she were my own, and I know in my heart how much that would have delighted her mother.

Although I think my husband was fond of the family, including the daughters – in fact he gave them both away at their weddings – there was always a feeling of detachment as though he was there because he had to be rather than because he wanted to be; maybe it was all part and parcel of the lack of intimacy between us, but we never talked about the girls' concerns, problems or futures together. To be part of their developing lives, careers, hopes, dreams, ups and downs gave me and still gives me immense pleasure, but I could never share that with my husband in any way, and to me this made the absence of their mother even more heartbreaking.

The loss of my close friend and confidante only increased my sense of isolation and I was determined not to involve the girls with my problems – they had suffered enough distress – and so the charade continued. I felt the girls needed to feel that their parents' close friends, whom they themselves had known since very small children, would always provide a place of safety and permanence for them, even though I knew the atmosphere of love that I tried to create for them was solely for their benefit.

The sense of detachment and distance to which I referred was brought into sharp focus shortly afterwards on the sudden and unexpected death of my own father. Apart from attending the funeral my husband made it clear that it was up to me to support my mother and arrange matters in general. Years later this attitude was repeated in relation to the sudden death of his father. Although obviously I was not involved then in the arrangements, the same dispassionate attitude was displayed when I broke the news to him as gently as I could. He simply responded, 'Well, it had to happen sometime.'

In relation to the death of my own father, owing to the distance that had widened between him and my brother, my mother made the decision – quite wrongly in my opinion – not to inform my brother of his father's death until after the funeral. I was extremely unhappy about this, believing my brother should have the opportunity to attend, but was told very forcefully by my mother that this was not only her wish but would also have been my father's, so my hands were tied.

The suddenness of my father's death distressed me greatly and I was immensely grateful for the opportunity to bid him a quiet private farewell in the chapel of rest. Years later, witnessing the agony of my mother's death, I am grateful at least that his departure was sudden with no such suffering.

It was obvious that my mother would need to move to a smaller house and she expressed the wish to move to a bungalow near to me. I therefore ceased working until she and I had sorted out all her affairs and had her happily settled a few miles away in a suitable property with a large garden, as gardening had become her all consuming pastime.

So within a year my mother was settled and I found another part-time job quite near her so I could call to and from work and generally be on hand for her when needed, as well as still being available for my husband, who although still working was by this time demanding even more attention. It was becoming obvious that he would be retired early on grounds of his disability, but for a few years we struggled on, as I felt he would be better working if possible for his own self-respect and sense of worth and well-being.

The next few years were quite a balancing act. The gentleman for whom I worked was charming and also had a slightly untypical home life, so we shared that together with a good sense of humour, without which I think we would both have been lost. My husband resented the fact that I had to spend time supporting my mother and my mother resented the inordinate amount of support and time I had to give my husband. She also became more aware and greatly concerned at the total lack of support and kindness that I was receiving from him.

When we both worked we were able to afford holidays but these were becoming increasingly difficult owing to my husband's moodiness and general lack of cooperation. We had self-catering breaks for a few years but even this became so difficult that in the end I refused to go any more. This was met with extreme displeasure, which he voiced in no uncertain terms to the consultant who, rising to my defence, said for me to take an already difficult situation into unfamiliar surroundings was quite intolerable. I remember feeling extremely grateful that someone actually seemed to understand in some measure how awful things were becoming. My husband, however, was enraged by this show of support for me and the journey home was not a pleasant one. However, holidays at least in that context were over.

Ultimately, my husband was duly retired early from his work, and the terms were favourable enough to ensure a safe future. At about the same time my employer decided to downsize his business for tax reasons. As my mother's health was beginning to give me cause for concern, it seemed an appropriate time to stop work so that I could devote my entire time to my mother and my husband.

Early one year I became very worried over my mother's poor recovery from what she insisted had been a cold. My mother did not accept interference readily, but I insisted she call her doctor and it transpired she had suffered a heart attack and was fitted with a pacemaker. Although the immediate problem was solved I was still unhappy about her overall demeanour but could elicit no information either to confirm any suspicions or allay my concerns. At the beginning of December I called early in the morning to find her lying by her bed, very hypothermic and obviously very ill. After having called for an ambulance I set about warming her, trying not to move her too much until I had assistance. In the course of my endeavours I discovered an enormous primary tumour on her left breast. It subsequently came to light she had been concealing this tumour since the July of that year.

She was admitted to hospital and never returned home. The cancer was extensive and untreatable. By January she had developed a secondary growth above her left eye, was blind, her weight was halved and it was only a question of time. Thankfully, with palliative treatment her distress until the last day was manageable. The fear she expressed to me and the Ward Sister, who fortunately was with me when she died, stemmed largely from when as a medical student she had witnessed a patient die in appalling pain from breast cancer.

The Sister and I assured her that with modern medical skills she would feel no pain when her time came, and with that assurance we seemed to approach the inevitable with some calmness. On the day of her death, in response to a call from the hospital, I arrived to find her obviously dying and in considerable pain.

Despite all the best efforts of the staff during the next 2½ hours my mother suffered pain and distress to a level that I hope I never witness again in a living creature. All bodily controls had been lost, together with her dignity, and with blind eyes she pleaded with me to end her suffering, reminding me endlessly that I had promised her no pain. Eventually, I said to the Sister that unless something was done to stop what was going on I would ask them to leave and I would deal with the situation myself. It sounds wrong now, but I would have smothered her with a pillow just to stop that suffering. The Sister knew I was serious and said she would have to leave for a few minutes. When she returned, with one injection my mother died within seconds in my arms. I sat with her for over an hour after she died and when I left that dreadful agony was still so etched into her poor contorted face that I insisted that my brother did not see her, but would remember her as she had been when he had seen her a few days earlier – very ill but nevertheless in relatively good spirits.

Walking into the car park to go home, I remember wondering how people could be going about as though nothing had happened – it seemed as though I had just visited a part of hell and then come back out into a different world. I bumped into a friend who asked if I was all right, as I think I must have looked pretty grim by then. I explained and she offered to drive me home, but I said I had my car and I had better get back. On arriving home and imparting the news of my mother's death to my husband, he said, 'Well, it's what you expected, wasn't it?'

That frosty winter's morning when I stood alone scattering my mother's ashes on the cold waters of the river, I thought that someday I would have to make some sense out of all this – I did not know how – but somehow I would have to try; otherwise, what would it all have been for? What followed only served to reinforce that resolve.

On my husband's retirement from work on the grounds of his ill health, I was advised to apply for disability allowance for him. I tried to involve him as much as possible in the process of completing endless forms and questionnaires, believing that he should be aware of and contribute to what was being said. I would try to obtain his cooperation, then write it all out in draft and go through it again to make sure it reflected what he wanted to say, then write it out again and ask him to read it. He was so truculent that I really wanted to make sure that he only signed something I knew he had read.

He was awarded a substantial monthly sum but in all the years he received it while he was at home I never put it towards the spiralling expenses we were incurring because of his disability, such as washing powder, an automatic chair, a new bed and necessary extra medical needs. Instead, I put it all towards him having some respite care away at the coast at a place of his choosing, so that he could have a change of scene and meet different people and have a holiday, and I too could have a break. Latterly I was so exhausted I did not bother with a break myself; just to have peace at home and time to clean the house, knowing that it would remain so for a while, was a break in itself.

Our general practitioner also realised the situation was becoming unmanageable and suggested my husband attend a day centre twice a week to give me a chance to rest and catch up generally. Very reluctantly my husband agreed to one day, and his resentment was palpable on each occasion.

It seemed somehow that I was the focal point of all resentment, so when for example it became clear to everyone that he should not drive it was my fault yet again, and I was accused of trying to take away his independence. If anything, it was *my* independence that was even more eroded as I dedicated myself to taking him wherever and whenever he wanted to go. I never had the house to myself and, more frighteningly, never knew what I would find when I returned home from walking the dog or from shopping.

On one occasion I returned from walking the dog prior to a planned weekly shop to find excrement wiped on the cloakroom wall and my husband sitting in his chair calmly reading the newspaper. When challenged he retorted he had 'been taken short' and that I had better clear it up before I went shopping: no other explanation, no apology.

Trying to ensure that he took his medication became a running battle as many small doses had to be taken through the day, and in an effort to maintain his independence I devised small containers all labelled for him or anybody who had to assist him, together with the smallest timer I could find. Thus he could be out all day, either when on respite or on the occasions when I would drive him to the nearby town to have some time on his own. Although the medics were impressed with my ingenuity, my husband dismissed it as useless and would frequently refuse to take his medication or on occasions throw it across the room.

I never knew when I came home what to expect, and that level of uncertainty, which quickly escalates into fear is, as anyone knows who has suffered it, exhausting. I would find soiled clothes hidden in drawers around the house, together with unstopped bottles of urine. Having difficulty passing motions is a common problem associated with his condition, but contrary to medical advice he would try manually to solve the problem. Then, refusing to clean his fingernails, he would eat a meal. I found him urinating in the middle of the bathroom in the middle of the night to be told it was nothing more than 'an oil leak'. Car seats and the cloakroom floor were soiled. The refrigerator door would be deliberately opened during the night, always on a day when I had done the shopping.

Many nights, too exhausted to undress, I have crawled onto my bed fully dressed with my dog and teddy bear next to me for company and a chair wedged against the door. I'd be too tired to sleep and too sad to cry, just grateful for maybe a few hours' relative sanctuary.

When embroiled in any situation of conflict, whether the setting is war or domestic conflict, the feeling of entrapment generated through a mixture of loyalty, duty and fear compels the participant onwards. Having signed up, so to speak, there is no way out or back, only forwards to see the task through to the end or as near to the end as possible; and although I did not know it, for me that end was approaching.

After considerable resentment and misgivings, my husband appeared to quite enjoy the respite breaks, and at least they gave me some small measure of freedom to be clean and to rest. Maybe it was these tiny glimpses of normality that began to awaken in me the realisation that the circumstances in which I was living were quite intolerable. It would have been difficult for me to believe then that they could get even worse. As was normal with my husband, the novelty value soon began to wear thin, and he made difficulties and would complain about going away. A locum doctor in our practice attended him and realised that his condition was becoming unmanageable at home and admitted him to hospital, explaining to me that the admission was as much for my benefit as for my husband's, as he realised that I was understandably near breaking point.

My husband spent five weeks in hospital, during which time his behaviour to the staff was polite and cooperative. He expected me to visit daily and would sit in the corridor so he would not be overheard. The change in his manner when a nurse approached with medication or the catering staff with his food, compared to his attitude to me, was both remarkable and revealing. It demonstrated to me so clearly that the bad behaviour was solely aimed at me; moreover he later told me he would only make an effort to behave if we had visitors because when they had left there was no one present who mattered. Later in the court proceedings he was to allege that all his bad behaviour had been caused by the disease from which he was suffering, but as I pointed out, after he had left and was living elsewhere none of that behaviour was occurring, although significantly he still had the disease.

As I say, during his hospital stay he cooperated with the medical staff, the welfare officers, physiotherapists and indeed anyone who might influence the decision that he could continue to be cared for at home or not. There was then arranged a meeting where all these good people, and my husband and myself were present. The purpose of this meeting was ostensibly to decide the best course of action for his future care.

Given his exemplary behaviour in hospital, any attempt I made to indicate how difficult the situation was at home was dismissed or ignored. For example, I was told it was demeaning to request him to wear incontinence pads, even though he had soiled car seats, carpets, ruined a bed and countless other incidents. He would not even allow me to put a mattress protector on the bed. I soon realised not least from the expression of satisfaction on his face that it was useless for me to pursue any other course than to accept that he would return home.

The Storm Breaks

So it was that we lurched on through another year, but that year was marked by a further eruption of the earlier violence, which forced me to think very long and hard about my future.

Respite and day centre visits continued but with increased resentment and thinly disguised aggression. Looking back now, I can map the escalation of this resentment into undisguised aggression. I was constantly being goaded, told I was worth nothing, nobody would want me, I would never get a job, if I left I would have nowhere to live and would have to have the dog put down. It went on and on, but I would not be provoked – even when on one occasion I was invited to push him downstairs!

When I discussed this with a very clever gentleman well versed in handling such situations, and expressed my abhorrence of violence particularly in a domestic situation, he explained to me that the behaviour had escalated into overt violence simply because I would not be provoked. Once provoked then a 'fight' is achieved. 'But what purpose does that serve?' I asked.

In my opinion, there's none, unless the purpose is to show a similar level of disrespect for life, as when a dog is beaten. However much I lack an orthodox faith, I have an immense respect for life. Within that context there are inevitably instances where war or merited punishment, properly reasoned and sensibly ordered, are part of life; but humiliation and abuse form no part of the structure, and are in themselves purely destructive.

There were numerous minor incidents of extreme aggression which although not involving actual violence nevertheless made me feel uncomfortable and vulnerable. Usually after he had gone upstairs to his room I would either sit in the garden or take the dog in the car and sit up on the common. He never knew I had gone; as long as his late night drink and medication were provided, I was of no interest to him anyway.

For me the final episode of physical violence came quite

unexpectedly and was quite literally terrifying. Having tried to make a calculation and finding it difficult to fathom, he asked me to look at it and I commented that I thought the decimal point was in the wrong place. The effect of this perceived criticism was sudden and dramatic; before I knew what was happening he was coming at me with such fury in his face that like a rabbit in headlights I froze, just managing to raise my arms to protect myself. He grabbed my wrists with such force that I had to struggle to free myself.

I realised it was not safe to stay, so I took my by now terrified dog and drove to a friend, who immediately suggested I call the police. This I now know I should have done, but at the time and with the turmoil in my mind I refused to do it. Like so many victims, I was ashamed and somehow in my mind everything that was then happening was my fault. Unless you have ever been unfortunate enough to be in such a position it is a very difficult attitude to understand, and is one of the many reasons why I am writing this book at all.

It is quite unacceptable to dump oneself on friends, however kind they are, with no realistic idea of your plans, so I knew I had to return. I telephoned in the morning to be told that nothing amiss had occurred and that he had restrained me because I was hysterical. As a very dear friend commented sometime later, if I had been hysterically inclined I would have murdered him years before. For the time being, however, I said I thought his behaviour had been unacceptable and we had to sort something out. He said he was going out but we could talk later. That 'talk' basically consisted of a diatribe, with him telling me that it had not taken long for me to come crawling back, which only served to support his contention that if I left I would have nowhere to go.

It is not difficult to imagine the atmosphere in the house after this. Maybe because his behaviour had not resulted in the 'fight' he wanted, but whatever reason his manner deteriorated even more. For days he would not talk at all, or he'd refuse his medication, sometimes leaving the house for hours with no explanation and then return to his room and refuse to talk or eat.

Another respite break was approaching, and as it coincided

with my birthday I had decided to have a few days away during his absence. A few days before he was due to go, as usual I took his morning tea and medication into his room for him and as usual got no response. I said his breakfast was all ready for him when he got downstairs, but that I was off to do a few bits of last minute shopping for his trip away; there was still no response, but I thought nothing of this as it had become the norm.

On my return from the shops about an hour later, he was still not up, so I went upstairs to find he had badly soiled the bed and was alternating alarmingly between total inertia and aggressive abuse. I called the surgery and eventually the ambulance, as I could not move him or get any sense from him at all. When the paramedic arrived together we managed to move him, change the bed and clean him up, whereupon he soiled everything again. However, he was politeness itself to the paramedic, and fulsomely appreciative of her help. He completely ignored me.

Finally we managed to get him settled, medicated and left him with a drink sitting up in bed watching the television. When we were downstairs I made the paramedic and myself a cup of tea while she filled out her forms. She turned to me and asked if I realised that my husband should be in care, and that there was no way I should be coping with a situation such as the one she had witnessed. She was so concerned by what she had seen that she asked if I would mind if she called into the local surgery on her way back, and left a message for the doctor.

The doctor called the next day and much against my husband's wishes insisted that he be admitted to hospital again that day. My doctor knew I had planned a few days away and made me promise I would still go, as with my husband in hospital there was nothing I could do and I must get some rest. After the doctor left the wait for the ambulance seemed interminable. My husband was so angry at everything, and I was beginning to find it difficult to make excuses for him any more, or to find it in my heart to forgive all those years of coldness and humiliation.

Finally the ambulance arrived, and he left with the bag I had carefully packed. He did not look back and I did not go with him. I spent the next four days washing and cleaning. I did not sleep much, nor did I allow myself to think because I knew I must sleep first. I visited my husband before I went away and found him still consumed with sullen resentment.

So I set off for a few days' break, during which I knew I had to decide what to do with the rest of my life and how much of that life I was still prepared to give to the person who had put me in this seemingly impossible position.

My first priority was to sleep, and this I did almost solidly for three days. Gradually I awakened physically and mentally, and in an atmosphere of safety and peace so long denied I began to reflect on what had passed and consider my options for the future. The disabling feelings of fear, uncertainty and fatigue that had for so long clouded any possibility of resolve or balanced decision making were beginning to recede and at long last I was able to think more clearly, although even then I did not realise how much longer it would be before my nightmare would finally end.

My first decision was that the situation as it had been was not going to continue. I had been advised from several professional quarters that my husband should be looked after in a care home where a succession of qualified people could attend to his increasing needs. From my perspective this seemed a sensible route to take, and so my next decision was to tell him on my return that either he would agree to go into care or I would divorce him. Either way, he could not come back to the house.

Although this must seem a very high-handed stance to take, I should explain that in all the thirty years we had lived in our house he had never shown any real sense of belonging – again the sense of detachment prevailed. Any improvements or suggested alterations, many undertaken for his benefit, had been met with a curious mixture of disinterest or opposition but never with optimism or enthusiasm. Despite all that had occurred, I loved the house and felt it to be my home in spite of everything.

My mother had left me quite a considerable sum of money which she had made in clear should be mine alone, although my husband apparently had no qualms in disregarding those wishes in the months that followed. However, it seemed there would be adequate funds to make either arrangement viable.

On my return I visited my husband and told him of my

decision. The time away had restored enough of my confidence for him to realise that my decision was final. Again, while in hospital – this time for nearly two months – his behaviour was without blemish, and another 'meeting' was suggested. The experience of the previous farcical debacle still very much in my mind, I expressed the view that if it was to be a repeat performance I did not see any useful purpose would be served, whereupon I was told that if there was no meeting then I would be on my own. As I had been effectively coping on my own for years this held no fear for me – even less now I had made my decision.

I told my husband that if he chose to go into care I would stand by him and make all the arrangements, both practical and financial. Furthermore, I would get work, so that together with his pension, disability allowance and our savings, including my inheritance, we should be able to afford his fees and for me to stay in the house.

Very grudgingly he accepted this suggestion in preference to divorce, and I set about making all the necessary arrangements. A care home was chosen, and I did everything I could to make his room as homely as I could with as many of his own things as possible. The staff at the home were wonderful and did everything they could to make him feel welcome, while maintaining as much independence for him as they could.

I visited regularly but on the advice of the home cut this back to twice a week to give my husband the opportunity to settle into his new life. Whenever I called, tea or coffee and biscuits always appeared as if by magic, and the staff were kindness itself, appearing optimistic that he had seen the sense in the compromise solution and would settle.

However, about two months after his entering the home he announced to me without warning that he had seen a flat he liked and that he intended to move out of the home and live by himself. To enable this to be done he demanded that I should dismantle all the financial arrangements I had made to fund the existing situation and make a substantial sum of money available to him, involving all our savings, on the basis that he would agree to the transfer of our house from joint names to my sole name.

Allowing for my mother's bequest, this did not represent a fair division, but he promised he would 'take this into account' when working out the final figures in relation to the remainder of our savings.

Although completely taken aback by this development, yet again I tried to see things from his point of view, and thought maybe he did need the opportunity to prove whether or not he could be independent. As had always been the case, there was no point in trying to have a reasonable discussion, so albeit with huge reservations in my own mind I reluctantly agreed to undo the financial arrangements I had made in order to raise the sum of money demanded.

I called on the Friday to tell him that the money required had been made available as requested. As it was a hot summer our meetings usually took place in the garden, and I was glad of this, having become very wary of being in confined spaces with him on my own. I told him that I had an appointment on the Monday to see a solicitor so that the transfer of the house to my sole name could be arranged as agreed.

Even after the passage of time, some events in a life remain vividly unforgettable and for me what occurred next is one such. Turning suddenly, he looked me full in the face with a look of such naked hatred and malice that I felt as if I had been struck. I will never forget the look in his eyes or the words he uttered telling me that he would see me in the gutter before I got the house, and if by any chance I did obtain the house he would destroy me by whatever means it took.

Again, like the rabbit in the headlights I sat momentarily stunned by what I had just seen and heard, and then quite suddenly I knew there was absolutely no point in trying any more. I rose, walked away, drove home and have not seen him again since that day.

My farewell to my boyfriend on Waterloo Bridge so many years before, the death of my mother in my arms, and now finally accepting that there are some people in this world you just cannot help however hard you try... As I said earlier in my story, the knowledge that a decision or course of action is the right one sadly does not always bring comfort or easing of pain. So it was with me on that drive home, but despite the pain I knew the end had come, and with that knowledge came what was almost a sense of relief that I no longer had to struggle against the impossible.

The appointment which was to have been concerned with transferring the house to my sole name became one of considering what steps should be taken to apportion and distribute the proceeds of a thirty-five-year marriage.

The flat was duly purchased, and I arranged to have delivered well over half the goods and chattels from the house. Apart from basic essentials, much of my home is equipped with the remnants of my childhood or items belonging to my late parents, and it has given me pleasure since to refill the gaps left with purchases from charity shops.

Despite numerous attempts and appeals from my own and his own solicitors, my husband refused to cooperate in providing necessary information and documentation, so after twelve months it became inevitable that the only way to progress matters was by way of court proceedings.

It would be inappropriate and invidious to go into the numerous manoeuvres aimed at me over the following year in relation to financial matters, threatening phone calls and sudden offers of settlement just as quickly denied; suffice it to say that his own solicitors (who ceased acting for him as soon as their duty was done) asked that their appreciation of the honesty and cooperation I had shown be communicated to me. As had been the case for so long, the disease which had sadly afflicted him for so long was being used to the full, both as a weapon and a shield.

Needless to say, the threat of losing the house and having to move away from a neighbourhood and community that had been my home for 3½ decades was daunting, particularly in the context of all that had gone before. My own health, which had already suffered from years of continual stress, deteriorated, and but for the love and support of friends, to which I have already referred and will refer to more later, finding the strength and determination to continue my struggle would have been well-nigh impossible.

On three occasions I have spent all night sitting quite calmly debating whether suicide would not be the best and most efficient way out for all concerned, provided my husband could not claim any part of what chattels I had left. This was the level of desperation to which all that humiliation and abuse had brought me, but again it was the love and concern of those whom I am proud to call my friends that won the day. What would they think if I took my own life? They would blame themselves for not having realised the depth of my despair, or felt themselves inadequate as friends that I had not turned to them for help; a poor legacy indeed to leave those who had shown me such kindness in such dark times.

Fortunately, on the day of the court case, my barrister was as efficient as the rest of my legal advice had been ineffectual, and did his best with the information he had been given. Although cognisant of my husband's ill health, the court was also made aware of my own and the not inconsiderable contribution I had made to the marriage both financially and practically over a long time. I had given only enough details of the abuse I had suffered to sustain a Petition for Judicial Separation, which was granted, but given the length of the marriage and all other factors of which the court were aware, I was awarded my home – at last, just over two years since the promise to make it mine had been so cruelly withdrawn.

For several months following the court decision I received a variety of telephone calls ranging from the pleading to the offensive. I tried to be patient during these conversations, reminding my husband that provided he obeyed the court order in relation to maintenance and medical insurance there was absolutely no reason for us to have any contact with each other, which would be for the best. He complained of having no friends and lacking my advice about administrative and other concerns. When at home, he would frequently tell me that I would be unable to cope without him – it seemed to annoy him intensely that perhaps the reverse was true.

During the whole of our marriage, no member of his immediate family ever lifted a hand to help me with him in any way. At his father's funeral, his mother rather begrudgingly expressed her gratitude for my having looked after him but, in thirty-five years, that was all. I felt then and feel now no obligation to be concerned with him or his family in any way whatsoever.

The storm had broken, the clouds were moving away and what I had to do was to find a life again. I had my home, although with very little money on which to live, and a wonderful circle of staunch and loyal friends; but what I had to do most of all before I could enjoy all these things was to find myself again.

Finding Myself Again with Laughter and the Love of Friends

The last three chapters of this narrative have been incredibly hard and painful for me to write. Three years after last seeing my husband, and having made an enormous effort to move on I was torn between my desire that the last forty years should and must serve some useful purpose and my reluctance to make myself relive the painful events so that I could accurately and fairly narrate them for the purpose of this book. Having nearly completed my task, I hope my reader believes that I have been true to the aims that I set myself – namely, to say enough of what occurred to serve the purpose but not just to recite a catalogue of woe and misdemeanours with a view to revenge.

Relationships fail, and few do so without acrimony at some level. But surely the sensible thing is to move on, accepting with as much grace as possible the outcome while still retaining respect for one's former partner as well as oneself. Maybe that is more difficult to do where one of the parties never felt that respect or affection, so the failure is not one of failing to secure happiness but rather of failing to inflict enough pain. Whatever the reason, I will never understand why or how a person can become so consumed with bitterness and antagonism towards the one person who is trying to care for them that they are driven to make that person's life a living hell.

My motive is not and never has been revenge. I did everything within my power to make my marriage work and I failed. I have to accept and deal with that perceived failure, from which standpoint I can then move on. And the writing of this book has been instrumental in that process and the rediscovery of my self.

I owe a huge debt of gratitude to many people so what follows may sound reminiscent of an acknowledgment speech at an Oscar Awards ceremony, but I make no apology.

First I must thank my parents, who brought me up with that code of values that has remained with me all my life – for better or worse. It was through them that my unusual upbringing endowed me from an early age with that strong sense of practical and emotional independence which came to my rescue in adulthood in a way I could never have foreseen as a little girl.

Next, my brother, who although rejecting many opportunities offered him must have felt curiously on the fringes of his family. He is now happily settled abroad and has thankfully found contentment and happiness at last.

During my marriage, much as I enjoyed the friendships I had and still have, it was difficult then to form close relationships. Feelings of shame, fear, uncertainty, isolation and a lack of self-esteem result in introversion. Anxiety about what awaits a homecoming inhibits the ability to concentrate on others. Later friends have said they suspected things were wrong but had no idea the extent of my distress. Now, so many of them have expressed pleasure at hearing me laugh again.

My father believed that the two best medicines in the world are sleep and laughter. I believe he was right, for having restored my body and mind somewhat with the benefit of sleep, laughter was then not so far away. A dear friend often quotes a saying she was given as a young woman: 'From quiet homes and first beginning, Out to undiscovered ends, There's nothing worth the wear of winning, But laughter and the love of friends.'

Certainly for me the love and support of my friends have enabled me to survive, and for that reason this book is dedicated to them. Not only have they believed me but they have also believed in me and my ability to come through these difficult times and find a way forward.

There have been so many kindnesses shown to me since I have been on my own, such as the friends who came to dinner acutely aware that finances were critical and arrived with enough fruit and vegetables to keep me going for months. Those same friends had over many years guessed at much of my predicament, and a permanent offer of sanctuary day or night was a great comfort to me as I knew it was genuine; telephone calls from friends around the country making sure I was safe and managing;

surprise presents for my dog to avoid embarrassing me with gifts when I was in no position to reciprocate; garden vouchers to finance either something for the garden or a cup of tea and toasted teacake as a treat. Several friends who grow their own vegetables keep me wonderfully supplied with in season produce, and I am often 'kidnapped' for a surprise lunch or morning coffee. Homemade cakes and tubs of soup frequently appear, and presents at Christmas and birthday come in useful vouchers for local food shops, so celebrations and festive seasons become more manageable.

Not least on my list of reasons to be grateful is the easy and natural inclusion of me into her family by the youngest daughter of my close friend. To watch her family grow, knowing how proud her parents would have been, gives me enormous pleasure and keeps the memory of that precious friendship fresh in my mind.

I must have the best and most supportive neighbours of anyone in the country, which was another important reason for my reluctance to move. They have supported me every inch of the way and in so many different fields, including their genuine happiness when they knew I would not be forced to move. I am immensely grateful to them all as I am to all my many friends without whose love and support I doubt I would have found the strength I needed. As with any of us, friendships are formed for so many reasons – during holidays, shared occupations or hobbies, similar interests, living next door etc. etc. Those who know me will agree that no account of my life would be complete without reference to teddy bears, and with them also comes a very large proportion of the friendships that I value so highly.

I have made periodic reference throughout this story to my father's rescued and restored teddy bear, Edward, and the comfort he has given me throughout my life.

Although now well over one hundred years old and therefore retired from strenuous duties, Edward has been with me from my earliest memories and is responsible for a lifelong interest and passion for teddies. Always with me he has shared my childhood, my school days, my years of student poverty and endless study, the dark years of my marriage, and the subsequent renewed poverty of little food and a cold house. But hopefully we are now embarking on happier and more peaceful times.

Over the years Edward has acquired numerous companions from far and wide. Some I have rescued and restored myself, thus learning something of teddy anatomy, which in turn led to my restoring for others and eventually to making my own. I also painted portraits of my family of bears and have been commissioned to do so for others, also writing the bears' stories to accompany the portraits.

This creative and satisfying hobby was crucial to my ability to cope with the situation I faced at home, occasionally allowing me to immerse myself in something completely separate from the relentless pressure under which I was obliged to function.

Many of the friendships I enjoy have been forged through bears one way or another, and sometime in the future it is my intention to compile a comprehensive and illustrated account of all my bears and their associations. It will be a much happier book and therefore an easier task than the present one now nearing its conclusion. However, it too will have a purpose – to support a firm belief already held by many that teddy bears provide a unique international language of love and understanding so much needed in the world today. For me they have been a much needed source of comfort and companionship, and watching fear evaporate from the face of a frightened child when presented with a teddy bear would surely convince and soften the hardest of hearts.

Maybe I dwell too long on the debt of gratitude I feel owe to all my friends, to my bears and my dog for helping me so much to come through such a long and difficult time, but I know without that support it would have been so much harder. It seems a long time since that cold February morning when I promised myself to make use of the pain I was feeling and to write this book to help albeit just one person, and it seems an even longer time since I made another promise to myself on my way back from London. I often wonder whether that young lawyer – not so young now, either – ever thinks of the young girl whose heart he broke and the course of whose life he altered for ever! I wonder what my parents would make of my application of the standards they gave me. Would they be proud or disappointed? I will never know, but I do know that I did the best that I was able with the life that I was given and will continue to do so.

Whatever my patient reader takes from this book, if it is in any way a sense of martyrdom or revenge then I have failed in my purpose. Despair comes in so many different forms and I know I have suffered far less than many, but the important message I have tried to convey is the same. Never let events destroy the innate trust in our fellow human beings which should be valued, not despoiled by the few. More than anything else I also know now that however bleak and hopeless a situation may seem and however tight the trap may feel, with a determination to survive and the support of those who love you adversity can be overcome.

I felt driven to write this book for those I could help, for my friends and for myself. Now it is complete I will embark on another book – a happy, light-hearted mystery adventure which will have some echoes of my childhood surroundings but none of the miserable years which I have now determined to put firmly behind me. Then of course, as my family of bears constantly remind me, I have their stories to tell, so hopefully we will enjoy future literary journeys together of a much more cheerful nature.

In the meantime, if you have travelled thus far with me, just believe and never *ever* forget that whatever life throws your way – there's always tomorrow.

If you enjoyed reading There's Always Tomorrow,
Emilie Defreyne's autobiography, then you may also wish
to read her first work of fiction:

Just What The Doctors Ordered (ISBN 978-1-909304-41-3)

And her latest novel:

Threading The Needle (ISBN 978-1-909040-56-4)